NOT MY OWN

A DEVOTIONAL LOOK AT GOSPEL APPLICATION

MATTHEW WATSON

WESTBOW
PRESS®
A DIVISION OF THOMAS NELSON
& ZONDERVAN

WestBow Press books may be ordered through booksellers or by contacting:

WestBow Press
A Division of Thomas Nelson & Zondervan
1663 Liberty Drive
Bloomington, IN 47403
www.westbowpress.com
1 (866) 928-1240

Scripture quotations taken from the New American Standard Bible®
(NASB), Copyright © 1960, 1962, 1963, 1968, 1971, 1972, 1973, 1975, 1977, 1995 by
The Lockman Foundation. Used by permission. www.Lockman.org

ISBN: 978-1-9736-9208-9 (sc)
ISBN: 978-1-9736-9209-6 (hc)
ISBN: 978-1-9736-9207-2 (e)

Library of Congress Control Number: 2020909508

Print information available on the last page.

WestBow Press rev. date: 6/5/2020

All of the song lyrics have been written by Janette … ikz and can be found on her *Not My Own* EP. All permission has been granted to use the lyrics as a part of this devotional.

This book is dedicated to my amazingly gifted daughter Amaris Mahogany. I pray that the Spirit opens the eyes of your heart, so that you may see the glories of Christ from a young age.

Christ rescues us from ourselves and trains
us, as He prepares us for home.
1 Thessalonians 1:9-10

Introduction

Not My Own: A Devotional Look at Gospel Application was created to draw individuals to a deeper place of devotion to the Christ. My wife created an incredible EP, *Not My Own*, and as a theologian and husband, I wanted to create literature that provided an extra level of accessibility to her art. I wanted people to be able to visually engage through reading as well as digging into the Word of God as a result of hearing my wife's music.

So this book is for those who love my wife's poetry and music and have been a part of her journey and ministry to the saints. This book is also for those who may have never heard of her before, since the book is written in a way where the portions of song lyrics are paired with scripture and the scripture is explained. This book is also for the one who is asking questions about who God is; those questions will be answered along with how you can come to know Him. Maybe this book was given to you as a gift and you don't know what to expect. If this is the case, you can expect to find out who the Creator of the universe is and the responsibility that you have before Him, both now and later.

I'm indebted to the Master's Seminary professors, their prayers, laying on of hands, teaching, admonition, and instruction. Without them I would not be as equipped for a lifetime of ministry in the Word of God. In particular, there is one professor who stepped in and became more for me. Dr. Paul W. Felix became like a father, and I am grateful for his wisdom, tenacity, humor, friendship, and discipline. Professor,

I have learned more from watching you and being a part of your life that I will ever be able to verbally express. I love you and am forever thankful for you.

This book is a deep dive into a method that I have spent nearly a decade compiling, as I sought to understand how to best convey incredibly deep spiritual truths in a simple way. I have come up with the five S's. These five S's are: Study, Significance, Survey, Supplication, and Solicitation.

Study is the first section where we skydive into the passage getting a quick overview of the surrounding context so that we can best understand our passage of interest.

Significance is the second section, where we take the understanding that we have gathered from the study section and properly apply it to understanding what that historical-grammatical means for us and how we should live in response.

Survey is the third section, where we probe ourselves with questions about where we are on our journey with the Lord and how intentional we are being about pressing forward to the higher calling to which we are being called. I was intentional about keeping this section small, because many times as believers, we have a desire to commit to something in a moment without truly being resolved about seeing it through. By keeping this short, our focus is better, and we are less distracted as we're seeking to apply biblical truth to our lives.

Supplication is the fourth section, where we pray to the LORD as we confess our sin that has been exposed through rightly understanding the passage and commit to following the LORD more intentionally with what we understand His requirement for us to be. It is important to note that this section could come off very offensive depending on where an individual may be on their journey with Christ. Sin is mentioned directly and terminology is used with reference to the holiness of the Lord. So instead of calling a particular sin a culturally accepted name, I stick with the names provided in scripture. As the author, I felt that this warning was necessary; as I would never want a perceived offense to become a hindrance to the proclamation of the glorious Gospel.

Solicitation is the final section and sends readers off to live out what they have just read and learned to apply. This section reads like the finale of a sermon and can lean in a few different directions based on what the passage prescribes. The passage could be leaning toward a petition or request type of sendoff or an imploring or demanding type of sendoff. The thrust of each passage is the determining factor.

This method has proved effective in my life and in the lives of countless others I have been privileged to teach and disciple. I believe this method to be so powerful because it allows for scripture to mean what it has always meant, while seeking to understand what that translates to in an individual's life. The end result of this process produces challenged convictions and readers asking deeper questions of themselves and their heart behind actions.

Filthy Rags and White Flags

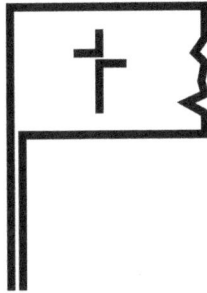

We do a lot of things, thinking that they are pleasing to God. It isn't until He introduces Himself that we begin to understand that we are unable to present ourselves to Him. There is no waiting and getting ourselves together when the timing is right. It's natural and prideful to think of our offering up to God and not see ourselves as desperate beggars in need of another's saving grace.

When captured by the Messiah, we are able to understand Him as our sole motivation and the source of all good that comes from us. It's at this place that we lose all other hope and see that hope itself is built on nothing more or less than Christ's atonement and righteousness.

I was created for the One that created and sustains all. I must let go of all that I hold dear and surrender.

For all of us have become like one who is unclean, And all our righteous deeds are like a filthy garment; And all of us wither like a leaf, And our iniquities, like the wind, take us away.

Isaiah 64:6, NASB

"You still see me,
Even though I stand here clothed in shameful leaves;
With nowhere to run and nowhere to hide
Umpteen thousand tries,
I'll be my own demise.
My pride, my lies, my mouth, my mind
Then you could press rewind …
My heart, my life, my eyes
Don't know why you love me.
Bloody murder, undeserving …"

Lyrics have been taken from the song, *Filthy Rags and White Flags* by Janette … ikz (Track 1, *Not My Own* EP)

Study

Isaiah records Israel's cry for YAH to hear them and relieve them of their adversaries. Isaiah knows GOD and realizes that He is fully able to relieve Israel of all of its adversaries in a moment's notice, but his appeal for Israel comes from a slightly different angle. It's an angle that is a familiar echo of many of the spokesmen for Israel. He doesn't appeal to YAH on the basis of them and their faithfulness, but rather, he appeals to the LORD to rescue His people on account His faithfulness to Himself—His namesake. The LORD is called upon to save Israel not because they are good, holy, obedient, or righteous. Israel was none of these! Israel had become entitled and felt as though GOD owed it to them to take care of them and continuously provide for them even in their unbelief and rebellion. They continued to live as though they were okay with Him, knowing that they were not. They had a form of GODliness and daily lived denying its power. So Isaiah includes himself in the representation of Israel by saying that their "good deeds" are absolutely powerless because they existed as workers of iniquity. The only thing that a worker of iniquity can do is call upon the name of the LORD to save them.

Significance

We unrealistically think that people are good. Since we are taught to believe this, as a societal whole, we try to find out how to bring out the good and selflessness that exists in everyone from birth.[1] But what if we have been approaching

---

[1] This is view that was popularized by the philosopher Jean-Jacques Rousseau. It has since been carried on to continue to be the most popular view of human nature.

the entire equation in the wrong way? What if we are just like Israel, in the sense that they thought they were naturally okay and without need of repentance because Yah had chosen to place His affection upon them? We fall into the same trap. We think because of our parents, our grandparents' pedigree, our position in society, our sphere of influence, or our social media following that we don't need repentance. There's no more contemporary of an example of this than when Donald Trump was asked if he needed to ask God for forgiveness. We don't think we need forgiveness because, while in our unbelief, we think we are all good. The truth is that none of us is good. We are born corrupt, and some take their wickedness to extreme levels. We are all in need of the one who can make us good, the one Israel looked for and awaited, and the one all of human existence centers around—the Christ of God, the Messiah.

Survey

What are some beliefs you have about yourself? What are some beliefs you have about others? Has scripture informed these views that you have about yourself and others?

Supplication

Confess your lack of study of God's Word and not relying upon God's abundant grace to grant wisdom in your time of need.

Commit to giving yourself over to steadily learning more of God's Word and to praying more about what the Lord would have you say and do.

Solicitation

Israel has been given to us as an example. They provide ways to follow after Y<small>AH</small>, and they provide a great deal of warnings for us too. It is our responsibility to learn the lessons the L<small>ORD</small> wants us to learn from scripture. Dedicate yourself before Him so that you may more faithfully know and serve Him.

I waited patiently for the Lord; And He inclined to me and heard my cry. He brought me up out of the pit of destruction, out of the miry clay; And He set my feet upon a rock making my footsteps firm. He put a new song in my mouth, a song of praise to our God; Many will see and fear and will trust in the Lord.

Psalm 40:1–3, NASB

"I was sinking deep in sin,
Very deeply stained within.
You're the Master of the sea,
From the waters lifted me.
You are God
You are King
You are Lord
My Everything,
You laid down Your life for me—
Rock, Salvation, Prince of peace!"

Lyrics have been taken from the song, *Filthy Rags and White Flags* by Janette … ikz (Track 1, *Not My Own* EP)

Study

David begins verse 1 of Psalm 40 recalling how his relationship with the Lord was not a rushed one. He reminisces upon a time where he was rescued by the Lord—but only after he waited upon the Lord. He indicates that while he was waiting upon an answer from the Lord, he was answered as YHWH "leaned in" to hear David and attend to him. The Lord was able to attend to David's cry because He actually heard him and perfectly knew his need. Yah spared David from a situation that could have been the end of him. We know that this was the case because David called it "the pit of destruction" or "the world of the dead." If this picture that David painted wasn't enough, he says it another way. He stated that he was brought up out of "miry clay" or muddy clay. He was completely covered and surrounded in a situation that seemed helpless when the mighty hand of the Lord carried him out. Upon the Lord's grasping of David, He takes him and places his feet upon a rock (which is symbolic of sure footing). The situation YHWH had just saved David from was anything but a secure foundation, and this showed David that when Yah saves, it's complete and total and lacks nothing. And David, the recipient, rightly caps this event of salvation with a song implanted in his heart. The Lord's secure protections against all odds causes His reputation to continue throughout the earth as many come to fear and trust in Him.

Significance

Most of the problems we have in life come as a result of our lack of patience. Whether it be financial issues, relational problems, or spiritual difficulties, it's usually as a result of our impatience. We don't like waiting for answers or results. We live in a society where we want *what* we want and we want it *when* we want. But we must know that there is one greater than us and all of our problems. Not knowing this simple truth makes life impossible, because everyone is constantly, internally reminded of how there are certain things we cannot do anything about. But it's in our internal struggles that we often neglect to cry out. This is what made David a "man after GOD's own heart." David is a proper view of self/ man and highly exalted praise for the Father. But many of our hang-ups can be found in our unwillingness to shout for help. Suicide is on the rise, and antidepressant prescriptions are at all-time highs, so it's obvious that there isn't a simple, natural answer to this problem that we face as humankind. The problem we face is much larger; therefore, we need to give it the one who has already taken all of the weight of the world instantaneously—the Christ of GOD.

Survey

Have you ever cried out to the LORD for salvation? Do you ever feel as though life is just simply too much for you? What do you do when you have emotions that cause life to be overwhelming for you?

Supplication

Confess your lack of prayer and crying out, your independence, your pride, and lack of humility.

Commit to praying more consistently and to turning to the LORD at all times, not just in time of trouble.

Solicitation

David has provided for us a testimony in holy scripture about the on-time GOD. We learn from this section that we are to be patient as we wait upon the LORD for His salvation. The LORD may not come when you want Him to come, but He is always on time. Being omniscient (all-knowing), He always knows when the rescue is right.

And He also told this parable to some people who trusted in themselves that they were righteous, and viewed others with contempt: "Two men went up into the temple to pray, one a Pharisee and the other a tax collector. The Pharisee stood and was praying this to himself: 'GOD, I thank You that I am not like other people: swindlers, unjust, adulterers, or even like this tax collector.'"

Luke 18:9–11, NASB

"I learned about the Law…
I need His mercy."

Lyrics have been taken from the song, *Filthy Rags and White Flags* by Janette … ikz (Track 1, *Not My Own* EP)

Study

Luke records a parable that the LORD uses to teach specific individuals a lesson. Luke places this lesson here because of its significance in tying together what He has just taught and what He will teach next. For Christ has just taught about how one comes to the faith, and now He's teaching, in our passage, what it means and does not mean to be of the faith.

Christ is going to teach this parable to people who trust in themselves that they are righteous. This means that these individuals trust in what their own hands accomplish for their acceptance before the LORD. Not only were these individuals self-righteous, but they also refused to look upon others. They felt that others were utterly worthless for not being like them. They were the standard, and those who were not like them were to be looked down upon.

Christ jumps into the parable by introducing two characters: a Pharisee and a tax collector. Surely those, trusting in themselves, listening to this parable being introduced would have thought great things were going to be said of the Pharisee because he was just like them. These two characters are introduced going into the temple to pray. The Pharisee's prayer is portrayed first. The Pharisee is pictured standing in a place of prominence in the temple that he may be seen. While standing in this position, he begins praying within his heart. His prayer is titled to GOD, but it is dedicated to self. He begins by thanking himself for not being like other people. If there was any confusion about what types of other people he was referring to, he lists them out. After completing his list of people that he keeps himself from being like, he adds on more praise to himself through his absolute disdain of the tax collector.

Significance

Self-righteousness blinds. As it blinds, it will blind in many ways. It causes people to not be able to see their own unworthiness. The inverse is also true of self-righteousness, as it cause people to see their own worthiness. Remember that the self-righteous are blind, so neither what they see nor don't see syncs with reality. Both seeing a worthiness that springs forth without God and not seeing that they desperately need Him just as much as the next man are both false depictions of the true faith that Christ has been presenting.

What we also see from this portion of the parable is that living self-righteously damages relationships with other people. This occurs because of what we stated earlier. They cannot award dignity to another because they are too busy awarding all of it to themselves for what they have been able to accomplish. It is as if they lose something if someone else gains, so they attempt to keep all praise for themselves—even while praying to God.

As obvious as Christ made finding self-righteousness in this parable, it can tend to be a bit subtler in our lives. It can show itself in how we may posture ourselves throughout life. How we tend to look at our growth in the Lord and tend to applaud our efforts or diligence. It can even show itself in the way that we seek to live lives that are set apart. Because if the way that you live set apart negatively looks upon your brother or sister in the faith, then that is self-righteousness.

It can be small things like seeing someone doing something wrong, but then missing the fact that you yourself do the same thing, maybe in a different way. Self-righteousness can also be in that secret place, where others cannot perceive it—your mind. No one knows our thought life except us, and that's the most dangerous part about it. Self-righteousness can show itself in all of these many ways and more, which is why we need to shore ourselves up with a community of believers who love the Lord and His Word and are committed to praying for one another.

I fast twice a week; I pay tithes of all that I get.

Luke 18:12, NASB (Part 2 of 4)

"I'm searchin' …
Tryna pay for what's already purchased.
Go to the service of 100 churches
To gain understanding on just how to earn this."

Lyrics have been taken from the song, *Filthy Rags and White Flags*
by Janette … ikz (Track 1, *Not My Own* EP)

Study

Luke continues to record the actions of this Pharisee from the parable Christ taught. The first continued thought that should be noted is how the Pharisee steadily points to his actions. As he points to his actions, he continues to give himself the glory for all that he points out. GOD received honorable mention in the verse prior, but here He isn't even cited. If we take note of what the Pharisee states, we will see he actually condemns himself in the ways in which he seeks to justify himself.

The Pharisee continues his soliloquy, stating that it is his norm to fast twice a week. This isn't something that is farfetched from a human perspective of understanding. It is also not a bad thing that he does, for fasting is a necessary and intentional part of the Christian faith. But the issue exists in the fact that he felt that all he did was in accordance with his strength and enablement. He knew nothing of understanding GOD's grace toward him.

Luke continues his record in maintaining that Christ illustrated that the Pharisee of this parable also made it his habit to pay tithes on all that he acquired. This, in like manner with the fasting, was above and beyond what was expected. The requirement was to pay tithes on all that you earned. He went beyond this by paying on all he earned and all he obtained (e.g., paying tithes on the money/resources you worked to gain; paying tithes on resources you get from spending the money/resources that you worked for and have already paid tithes on). This would be great for someone to do, but the thing is that doing this could not ever make a person a member of the faith.

It's incredible that the entirety of this self-righteous prayer is actually doable. But this is exactly Christ's point: *doing* anything will never be enough. Redemption and becoming a member of the faith takes more than what any normal person could ever *do*. This is the condemnation that the Pharisee of this parable brings upon himself. He wants to be justified by his actions, but these self-righteous actions are actually his condemnation.

Significance

We must notice something that was identified earlier, which is that sin is a matter of the heart. I cannot emphasize this enough. Because Christianity isn't a list of dos and don'ts, but it's a loving relationship with the one who gave it all, that you might be in right relationship with Him. The Pharisee's issue is that he sought to justify himself with his actions, and many times we seek to do the same thing. Of course, we don't announce it as such, but when we examine our motive, that is indeed what we will find. It's not that an action itself is bad; more so, we often get ourselves in trouble because the action wasn't bad, but our heart motives were. We must constantly remind ourselves that we are nothing without the LORD's strength and enablement. GOD's common grace even allows for the unbeliever to have a level of stick-to-itiveness to remain dedicated and committed to accomplishing tasks. We also have to train ourselves that self-righteousness condemns. We lie to others and cheapen GOD's grace and strength when we exaggerate where we are spiritually. We don't lie to ourselves though, for we are fully aware of where we truly are.

Survey

Do you question yourself on self-righteousness? Do you know how to question your heart? Do you believe that you could be self-righteous in certain ways? What does your fight against self-righteousness look like?

Supplication

Confess your pride, your self-righteousness, your improper view of self and others, and improper view of GOD.

Commit to thinking rightly of self, to believing properly of others, and praying for the forgiveness that you need daily.

Solicitation

We learned that self-righteousness is sin and that it can easily overtake us if we are not careful. We also learned of some of self-righteousness's deceptions can even find their way into our prayer life if we do not extinguish them as they arise. We must understand that the LORD is our source, and we can accomplish nothing without Him.

But the tax collector, standing some distance away, was even unwilling to lift up his eyes to heaven, but was beating his breast, saying, "God, be merciful to me, the sinner!"

Luke 18:13, NASB (Part 3 of 4)

"I learned about the Law,
Broke one so I broke 'em all.
It's a shame, I'm so guilty
And my pockets are so empty.
I could never ever pay,
For all the depravity on my plate …
I need His mercy."

Lyrics have been taken from the song, *Filthy Rags and White Flags* by Janette … ikz (Track 1, *Not My Own* EP)

Study

Christ continues His parable with our formal introduction to the tax collector. Our introduction to him comes with strong contrasting language that helps us to know that he will be different than the Pharisee we just finished reading about. Christ says that he was standing some distance away within the temple. This comparison of where he is standing isn't necessarily with the Pharisee, but rather with everyone else who would have been in the temple at that time. We read a couple verses prior that the Pharisee took a prominent position within the temple that all others wouldn't have been able to take. So this tax collector takes a position that is some distance away from the others. If his described positioning wasn't enough, he is also described as not being able to lift his eyes to heaven. This is a direct indication of his understood unworthiness. Christ depicts him even further as continuously beating his breast. In his prayer to the Lord, he cannot stop beating upon his chest in contrition. The words he spoke were simple and poignant. He acknowledged his need as a sinner and recognized the Lord as the only one able to do something about his condition. He asked that the Lord would be gracious and propitious toward him.

Significance

The Lord lays out for us the perfect way for us to present ourselves before Him. We are to come to the Lord humbly, understanding that only He is worthy. This is the prerequisite to salvation. We must come to the Lord repentant and contrite. For if individuals seek to come another way, they show themselves to be just like the Pharisee. The striking reality about humbly seeking after the Lord is that He picks those first who are traditionally picked last. Maybe you're aware, or maybe you aren't, but being a tax collector was not a profession that was looked upon favorably. Tax collectors were known to cheat and take advantage because they had the Roman government on their side. But before we judge too quickly, we all have things that we need to cry out to the Lord for mercy in. That's the thing—we all come asking that the Lord would be merciful, and we all stay continuously asking that the Lord be merciful. No one should ever allow him- or herself to be deceived in thinking that this isn't the case. For everyone who is genuinely of the faith knows that there are many ways they can grow in faithfulness to Christ.

The incredible truth about presenting yourself before the Lord is that He is so fair that everyone who genuinely comes leaves with what they came looking for. It doesn't matter whether it's your first time and you're coming to be justified—He'll do that. It doesn't matter if it's your umpteenth time and you are crying out to the Lord for a renewed strength—He'll do that. He is always ready to forgive, because He knows of our desperate need of Him. So don't ever be ashamed to cry out to Him for help.

Survey

How would you describe the way you go before to the Lord in prayer? Is your prayer time intentional? Is your prayer time repentant? Do you understand how much you need the Lord's enablement moment by moment? Are you afraid to verbally express your need of the Lord?

Supplication

Confess your lack of humility, your lack of contriteness of spirit and not crying out to the LORD.

→ not arrogant

Commit to living unassumingly in your relationship with the LORD, to confessing freely to the LORD, and to acknowledging the LORD's graciousness.

Solicitation

We are not to exalt ourselves in our own eyes; neither are we to seek to exalt ourselves in the eyes of others. Both of these practices are detrimental to our spiritual health. Rather, we are to have a sober assessment of ourselves in knowing our need of the LORD's grace.

What do you need to repent of.

I tell you, this man went to his house justified rather than the other; for everyone who exalts himself will be humbled, but he who humbles himself will be exalted.

Luke 18:14, NASB (Part 4 of 4)

"I surrender my life to the One,
Who drank all of the cup,
The High and Lifted Up—
He got up!"

Lyrics have been taken from the song, *Filthy Rags and White Flags* by Janette … ikz (Track 1, *Not My Own* EP)

Study

Christ ends the parable here in this verse, as he explains the results. We know that the parable was given to those who trusted in themselves for their righteousness. We see that He ends the parable by showing them how they indict themselves with their actions. He goes on to state that the tax collector goes to his home justified and the Pharisee does not. This would have shaken them to the core, as it represents the exact opposite viewpoint from the one that they taught and lived. But this is exactly the reason for the parable being delivered to them. They couldn't understand that being of the faith wasn't attached to who their forefathers were; rather, it was entirely based on the individual's relationship with the one true God. They thought that they could do the work of initially cleaning and keeping themselves clean, but they didn't understand that the task they set out upon was impossible. Christ ends the parable with a familiar proverb about humility. He communicates to them the truth that the self-righteous will be quickly awakened to the reality that they are not righteous, while those who understand their need and cry out will have their need met. He is teaching that there can be no righteousness to be found without humility.

Significance

What we must take away from this parable is that there is no way anyone can self-righteously stand before the Father in this life or the judgment that comes after. The only way a person can be presented as justified before the Lord is in receiving the mercy that He has given to the world in the person of Christ. All of the attributes we seek to pronounce upon ourselves are perfectly found within Him. That's the chief problem with self-righteousness: it seeks to reduce the Lord's glory and minimize the work accomplished in humans by way of the Holy Spirit. This is entirely unacceptable to the Lord, as He has revealed plainly throughout scripture that He will share His glory with no other.

This is why the parable ends the way it does. If we improperly desire the Lord's glory, which we have established does not and will never belong to us, He has to bring us low in order for us to rightly live in proper respect to His majesty. But for those who properly and accurately attribute to Him what He is due, He lifts those individuals up. Many times it may not make sense to us why the Lord may exalt a certain individual over another, but that's not for us to try to figure out. Being the loving Father that He is, He knows perfectly what each one within His creation needs. This is why He is to be the recipient of all of our trust.

Survey

Have you been declared righteous? How do you know that you have been declared righteous? Do you continuously seek the Lord to walk daily in righteousness?

Supplication

Commit to trusting in the Lord's justification and living in humility.

Solicitation

Since we desire the Lord's approval against that of men, our responsibility is to ensure this by not focusing on lifting ourselves in the eyes of humans. In some ways, this is easier said than done, but humility is a process that you improve over time with consistent work. We should not neglect humbling ourselves, as this is the only way by which we may see the Lord.

Not My Own

If you are a believer, you must show this to be the case with thoughts, words, and actions. You are to be submitting yourself to the spirit of GOD that has chosen to make your heart His dwelling place, as you bow down in worship. Every aspect of your life is to be approached as worship.

Understand that you are His instrument, and being used by Him is where you have value and find your worth. Outside of the Messiah's use, life is futile at best. Resolve to pursue Him, instead of what He has created.

I was created for the glorification of my Creator, not myself.

Or do you not know that the one who joins himself to a prostitute is one body *with her*? For He says, "The two shall become one flesh." But the one who joins himself to the Lord is one spirit *with Him*.

1 Corinthians 6:16–17, NASB (Part 1 of 4)

"This feels like Eden.
The Eve in me craves and thirsts
To take heed to the snake that works,
To make beef between me
And the speech of the Creator,
So it grieves me to say yes sir!"

Lyrics have been taken from the song, *Not My Own* by Janette … ikz (Track 2, *Not My Own* EP)

Study

We come in to Paul's first letter to the Corinthians, with him explaining in detail for them that how they live matters to the LORD. What you see in reading the surrounding chapters is that the Corinthian church was getting involved and entangled in matters that were irresponsible for them as believers. Paul's point is that the way that they were living was giving a bad reputation to the household of faith.

So in keeping with this same theme, Paul speaks on the topic of immorality. In verse 17, where we find ourselves today, he uses the same exact language for being joined to a prostitute and being joined to the LORD. He does not equate them in the sense of saying they are the same, but he's equating them from the framework of understanding that you are one with the one to whom you join yourself. Explained further, to sleep with a prostitute (v. 16), you are physically joined to her, but we need to understand the spiritual connection that takes place as well. Physically, there is a oneness that takes place that cannot just be left as one isolated act. The act committed causes there to be a union, as the two have become one flesh. Greater than simply using these words, we need to look at the author of these words Paul quotes—the LORD. The LORD has established that physical intimacy causes the participants to become one. This means that lasting effects cannot be avoided because of the union.

On the other side, Paul teaches that there is a spiritual joining that takes place in our relationship with the LORD; but it would be terribly foolish to neglect properly understanding the physical connection that goes along with this. The spiritual connection is defined in many different ways throughout the Bible, but suffice it to say that Christ is our spiritual representation before the Father. This spiritual aspect is paired with the physical expectation that we will operate in self-control in view of this new reality. This is why Christ and the New Testament writers reiterate the same point in different ways about our will no longer being the priority of our lives.

Significance

We are not the first impure culture, and you can rest assured that we will not be the last, unless the LORD makes His imminent return. Everything we can spend our time actively pursuing, with the exception of getting to know the LORD, will leave humankind without resolve. This is why humans, during their short time here on this earth, must come to understand that we have the responsibility to be intentionally seeking after the LORD on a daily and continual basis. This being said, Solomon teaches us in Ecclesiastes that there is no task that can fulfill humans in the way that we desire fulfillment and that the LORD has made this purposely the case. To quote the wisdom given to him from the LORD directly:

> All the rivers flow into the sea, yet the sea is not full. To the place where the rivers flow, there they flow again. All things are wearisome; man is not able to tell *it*. The eye is not satisfied with seeing,
> Nor is the ear filled with hearing. That which has been is that which will be, and that which has been done is that which will be done. So there is nothing new under the sun. Is there

anything of which one might say, "See this, it is new"? Already it has existed for ages, which were before us. There is no remembrance of earlier things; and also of the later things, which will occur, there will be for them no remembrance among those who will come later *still.*
(Ecclesiastes 1:7–11 NASB)

Solomon understands that everything in this world is vanity, and nothing will provide what it promises. We miss this central truth of life because of our lack of diligence to know what was before us. Many times our desire to learn is improperly motivated. When this happens, you can *know* something and have absolutely no idea about it at the same time. This is what was happening within the Corinthian church and still happens within the church today. Someone is converted on Sunday but is without knowledge for what it means for Monday. Many times we are spiritually defeated because we aren't submitting ourselves to our Savior, who has already won the victory on our behalf. But when we truly come to understand that we do not belong to ourselves, our lives are purified physically and spiritually. We physically do different activities and refrain from other activities that we used to participate in; while spiritually, we commit ourselves to the actions that we have been called to carry out for our growth. But because of our neglect of what the LORD has instructed, we often spend too much of His time wasted as we refuse to learn the lessons He is teaching us. Because the truth of the matter is that we still fight to belong to ourselves. When we cease striving, we come to know His grace in an entirely new way.

Flee immorality. Every *other* sin that a man commits is outside the body, but the immoral man sins against his own body.

1 Corinthians 6:18, NASB (Part 2 of 4)

"I am not my own
I belong to Him!"

Lyrics have been taken from the song, *Not My Own* by Janette ... ikz (Track 2, *Not My Own* EP)

Study

Paul continues his thoughts by saying that the Corinthian believers had an obligation to stay away from immorality. Paul warns them to never commit immorality. He says that every sin is outside of the body except for this type of sin. What did he mean when he said this? Paul is expressing that out of all of the other sins that can be committed, the sin of immorality affects the human more intensely. Paul isn't ranking sin, which we know that the Bible doesn't teach; what Paul is doing is teaching these believers that certain committed sins will have lasting effects on the one who commits them—even their bodies. When you begin to think of sins that you can commit (e.g., drunkenness, laziness, hatred of God, lying, etc.) Paul's point becomes all the more clear. All sin takes an effect, but the sin of immorality has a greater effect on an individual long term. Immorality produces negative long-term physical, spiritual, or emotional/mental effects. This is why Paul uses the strong language that he does when he is telling them to run away from it. This is why the Proverbs state the naivety of the one who still decides to rush in even though they are aware that nothing good can come of the situation and grave danger is guaranteed.

Significance

We put ourselves in unnecessarily dangerous situations, and many times it is not by accident. It's as if we enjoy the rush of potentially not making it out or experiencing the nearness of not making it out, only to escape at the last moment. Paul teaches that the LORD will provide a way of escape for us, but the problem is that as a result of the kindness of the LORD, we end up being presumptuous of His graciousness. He looks out for us in so many ways that we couldn't ever imagine it working out any other way.

When we think of all that Paul spells out in this verse, we also come to understand that he is teaching that it is irrational to commit immorality. It is not a normal for an individual to want to sabotage oneself. We've discussed many ways in which this self-sabotage could occur, but one very obvious complication to add to the list of problems already discussed is that of disease. Disease was commonplace among those who lived immorally; even with modern technology and medicine, the same is true today. This is why, as believers, we should be living lives that show that we care for the LORD's investment. This is why it should be our desire to prove His depositing of the Spirit within us was not a waste. He knows this, but we need to prove this to ourselves.

Survey

Is it your habit to flee temptation? If so, what is the motivation? If not, why are you not motivated to flee temptation? Are you aware of the consequences of your union with Christ? Are you aware of any ways in which you self-sabotage?

Supplication

Confess acts of intentional sin and refusing the Spirit of GOD.

Commit to forsaking intentional sin and fleeing immorality.

Solicitation

It's clear that in our unbelief, some of us have committed some atrocious acts. Paul's point here is that was a representation of who we once were, but we were justified by Christ's accomplishment and the application of the Spirit (v. 11). Since this is the case, we have a responsibility in our oneness with Christ to act accordingly, for we are one Spirit. He has already provided the power to overcome in time of weakness; we simply have the responsibility to access it. Will you access it?

Or do you not know that your body is a temple of the Holy Spirit who is in you, whom you have from GOD, and that you are not your own?

1 Corinthians 6:19, NASB (Part 3 of 4)

"I am not my own,
I belong to Him
I am not my own,
I belong to Him!"

Lyrics have been taken from the song, *Not My Own* by Janette … ikz (Track 2, *Not My Own* EP)

Study

As we read Paul's words introduced by rhetorical device, we get a chance to see that he is leading them to truth that has been before them with an application to life that has been missing. He begins their trek by reintroducing a concept that had already been taught and addressed. He's calling on them to truly grapple with the idea of accepting and taking ownership of the fact that the Holy Spirit lives within those of the household of faith. Paul announces this idea when he states that the believer's body is a temple of the Holy Spirit. He's teaching them that the Spirit is what makes them a dwelling place and a sanctuary. For the Spirit of God makes and keeps one holy, and it is impossible to have holiness otherwise. Paul's appeal to the Corinthians' sanctification was also on the basis of the plan of God. He's teaching them that they needed to be holy, because this was God's plan in choosing them. He gave them the gift of His Spirit to live within them so that they would live holy lives dedicated unto Him. This is why the connecting thought "you are not your own" is delivered the way it is. Paul had, in many words, expressed to them that they didn't have the right to do what they wanted to do; but at this point, he appeals to the highest authority—the Lord. He tells them that they belong to the Lord. Said another way, they are the Lord's property and possession. This is why they were to seek, by the Spirit's enablement, to live holy before the Lord.

Significance

As we have seen, Paul's questioning statements are more statement than question. In doing this, he brought to the

Corinthians' attention the reality of the need for theology to be lived out.

He begins with the idea of the Spirit living within the believer bringing two dueling realties into play. The first reality is that the Spirit of GOD comes with the aiding ability to help us in our fight to remain holy; but the other side of this same coin is the reality that we can grieve the Holy Spirit with our sin and lack of holiness. This means that the reality of the Spirit of GOD making us a temple is to entirely have an impact on our conduct.

Looking at the reality of the picture that Paul has painted, there are just certain things you wouldn't do in a temple because a sanctuary is, well, sanctified. It's clean and pure. This is Paul's point; when the things you want to do defile you, remember that you do not belong to yourself, because you have been made a temple by the Father, and the Spirit now lives within you.

Therefore, sanctification should not be seen as optional for the believer in the LORD.

Survey

Are you aware of GOD's plan for you? What reverence do you give to the Spirit of GOD that lives within you? Are you aware that you are unable to do whatever you want to do whenever you want to do it?

Supplication

Confess not living as a temple, not honoring the Holy Spirit living within you, and forsaking God's plan for you.

Commit to living as a temple, to God's plan for you, and submitting your desires before the Lord.

Solicitation

There is a requirement upon every believer to live in a way that is pleasing before the Lord. The scripture is filled with this testament. As believers, each of us has to make up our mind that we are going to live uprightly and resolve to this end. Settle for nothing less; Christ did. Just as He submitted Himself to the Father's plan, we too must do the same, because we are neither the master of our fate nor the captain of our ship. So we will freely offer ourselves unto our Master.

Sunsafey: moms stressed

For you have been bought with a price: therefore glorify God in your body.

1 Corinthians 6:20, NASB (Part 4 of 4)

"I know the Pilot, but
I am here gluing these feathers—
Thinking I'm doing it better."

Lyrics have been taken from the song, *Not My Own* by Janette …
ikz (Track 2, *Not My Own* EP)

Sin causes all of the things we talked about earlier, but there is one who loves perfectly. There is one who knows better than we ever could what is best for us. There is one that we are to gratefully give the entirety of ourselves to, knowing that He has never failed or made a mistake. We should be appreciative as we navigate through understanding how indebted we are in relation to Him. Because what we have to keep in mind at all times is that His purchase of us was expensive. It wasn't because we were worth it but because in belonging to Him, we have acquired a worth that is far beyond what we could ever grasp. So glorifying our Master should be seen through the lenses of utter thanksgiving for being chosen to belong to Him.

Survey

Do you know the price that has been paid for you to have life? Do you seek to glorify GOD with all of you?

Supplication

Confess your lack of gratefulness and not fully trusting in the LORD.

Commit to growing in submitting yourself more to the LORD.

Solicitation

Everyone who knows the LORD in a saving way knows what has been accomplished on his or her behalf. In knowing this truth, we should never allow it to become so common to us that we lose our heartfelt appreciation. Challenge your soul daily to seek to give to the LORD that which He is due. All glory is due unto Him and no other. Let us choose continually, each day, to give Him what we owe Him—our very being.

But you are a chosen race, a royal priesthood, a holy nation, a people for GOD's own possession, so that you may proclaim the excellencies of Him who has called you out of darkness into His marvelous light; for you once were not a people, but now you are the people of GOD; you had not received mercy, but now you have received mercy.

1 Peter 2:9–10, NASB

"You are a flute that is mute as an instrument;
You can't be sound if He does not blow into it."

Lyrics have been taken from the song, *Not My Own* by Janette … ikz (Track 2, *Not My Own* EP)

Study

We come to this text as Peter is in the heart of his argumentation for those residing as aliens in modern-day Turkey. He's writing to them, encouraging them to live rightly before the watching world around them and to suffer well, knowing that future glory awaits them. In the verses that we will be examining, Peter has just finished speaking about the disobedient and their rejection of the Messiah and how there is a judgment awaiting all of those who choose to reject Him to the point of their death. He then sharply contrasts this with those who believe and live in obedience.

In verse nine, Peter appeals to the Old Testament, which is something that he has done a lot in this letter. He's proving the connection of these Christians to the OT passages that spoke of the same truth, to teach these dispersed Christians who they are. He's teaching them through OT passage quotations that they are GOD's people, because of His selection of them. Peter states that His purpose for choosing them is that all of the ones chosen would proclaim to the entire world the greatness of the Most High. Peter also compares these immigrants to Israel from an additional angle.

He states that they were nothing and the LORD called them His people and He made them a great people. They had been the pity of others and were lifted by Him and were to extend the mercy that they had received to the others who had not yet professed faith in the LORD.

Significance

Naturally, coming to the place of understanding that you have been chosen can be emotionally overwhelming. You may start off with this overwhelming sense of gratitude because you realize you are so undeserving. These feelings lead to dramatic service because of a steady growing knowledge of all that has been accomplished on your behalf. This can then lead to a sense of pride because you begin to realize all that you do on behalf of the LORD and that everyone that belongs to Him isn't serving Him as fervently. This can then lead to an entirely different sense of being overwhelmed than the beginning because you began to examine what you do on behalf of the LORD, and you begin to construct a picture of why the LORD chose you. But I must warn you to destroy this picture immediately, because there is no truth to it. The LORD didn't choose you *because of*, but His choice of you comes *in spite of* you. This is true for all of our brothers and sisters who have come before us—even the ones we admire so much. The veracity of scripture proves this to be the case, as we see even their low points of life contained for us to read and learn from. Humility of thought and thinking properly of self is indeed a hard truth to grapple with, but we must acknowledge it as the truth.

We must never lose the zeal that has caused for us to come to the faith that we now know. The LORD has chosen to be gracious to us and for that our lives should forever show our gratitude.

Survey

Are you aware of what the LORD says about your status as a believer in Him? Does this knowledge provoke a greater faithfulness from you? Do you seek to represent the Lord in every way that you know possible? Do you consistently rehearse the truth that the Lord gives you your identity, so that it isn't searched for in any other place? How is your life different as a recipient of mercy?

Supplication

Confess not living up to the standard by which you have been called, not proclaiming the greatness of the Lord, and complaining about circumstances that the Lord allows.

Commit growing in better understanding what the Lord requires of you, intentionally complaining less, and speaking more about the Lord's goodness.

Solicitation

We have experienced a transformation that the world needs to know about and that the people who know us personally have faced alongside of us. This is why we have a responsibility to intentionally speak about what has occurred. We have become great because of our adoption by the greatest of all time. Being in His family is the greatest success our lives will ever attain. This is why we should be spending more time telling His story than our own. For our greatest triumphs are nothing in comparison to what He has done within us.

Then Jesus came with them to a place called Gethsemane, and said to His disciples, "Sit here while I go over there and pray." And He took with Him Peter and the two sons of Zebedee, and began to be grieved and distressed. Then He said to them, "My soul is deeply grieved, to the point of death; remain here and keep watch with Me." And He went a little beyond them, and fell on His face and prayed, saying, "My Father, if it is possible, let this cup pass from Me; yet not as I will, but as You will."

Matthew 26:36–39, NASB

They came to a place named Gethsemane; and He said to His disciples, "Sit here until I have prayed." And He took with Him Peter and James and John, and began to be very distressed and troubled. And He said to them, "My soul is deeply grieved to the point of death; remain here and keep watch." And He went a little beyond them, and fell to the ground and began to pray that if it were possible, the hour might pass Him by. And He was saying, "Abba! Father! All things are possible for You; remove this cup from Me; yet not what I will, but what You will."

Mark 14:32–36, NASB

And He came out and proceeded as was His custom to the Mount of Olives; and the disciples also followed Him. When He arrived at the place, He said to them, "Pray that you may not enter into temptation." And He withdrew from them about a stone's throw, and He knelt down and began to pray, saying, "Father, if You are willing, remove this cup from Me; yet not My will, but Yours be done."

Luke 22:39–42, NASB

When Jesus had spoken these words, He went forth with His disciples over the ravine of the Kidron, where there was a garden, in which He entered with His disciples.

John 18:1, NASB

When He had spoken these words, He went forth with His disciples over the ravine of the Kidron, where there was a garden, in which He entered and His disciples. He went a little further, about a stone's throw, away from them and knelt down on the ground and fell on His face and prayed that if it were possible, the hour might pass from Him. And He said, "Abba, Father, all things are possible for you. If it is your will, take this cup away from Me; nevertheless not my will, but Yours, be done."

Matthew 26:39; Mark 14:36; Luke 22:42, NASB

"But I've learned that
You have two eyes but His
Foresight is infinite.
Trust in the LORD and lean not on your sentiments."

Lyrics have been taken from the song, *Not My Own* by Janette … ikz (Track 2, *Not My Own* EP)

Study

In covering the description from each of the synoptic accounts, we see fully what took place as we examine Christ's prayer in the garden of Gethsemane.

When noting the location of this prayer, it's cited as being right after Christ had just finished praying. The prior occasion of prayer reveals Christ to pray strength, joy, and encouragement for Himself, His disciples, and all who believe in Him.

After praying the prayer of the entire chapter of John 17, Christ takes His disciples inside of a garden of olive groves at a place called Gethsemane, which is a place where He regularly met with them. He took Peter, James, and John with him deeper into the garden of groves, where He began to feel greatly grieved and distressed. He leaves the three here and asks them to remain there, but to be watchful and pray. The text reads that, "His soul is deeply grieved, to the point of death." So it's truly noteworthy to see Him needing the strength, for He prayed immediately after praying it.

So Christ goes even deeper into the garden to pray, and at this point, He is about a stone's throw away, and the words He prays to the Father are going to be our focus.

Christ kneels down and takes His face to the ground and begins to pray. He begins His prayer with an identification of His closeness with the Father. He uses this moment to reflect upon not drinking the cup of suffering; but we see immediately from the recorded account that He calls His soul to not focus on His own desire at this time, but the will of the Father. Christ wants the will of the Father to be done.

Significance

Looking at the representative verses, from each gospel account, together a full picture is born. This full representation humbles our soul as we get to see our Messiah accepting the will of the Father and the struggle and angst He faced. Many times, when we think of this prayer, we can take it too far in either direction. We can either make Him too human or too holy. We have to be careful to represent Him exactly as Scripture does. Say everything that Scripture says and what Scripture does not say; don't say that it does. Christ being too human is to say that He begs so hard in the garden and never gets to a place of truly accepting the will of the Father, but because of formality, He just goes through with it anyway. Making Christ too holy is only referencing many who make it as though His suffering wasn't real and that He didn't feel anything. It's as if the events the Bible records happened, but they just really didn't happen to Him. This isn't honest to what scripture teaches or represents. It's at the image of the hypostatic union that we marvel. Our Christ is fully both. He's fully aware of the struggle of the human condition and human limitation, while at the same time our perfect representation and high priest before the Father.

We are also able to see Christ's wisdom as He goes to pray in the garden. He takes all of His disciples, but as He goes deeper into the garden, He only takes Peter, James, and John with Him and asks them to keep watch and pray with Him. He knew the importance of asking that others would pray for Him. A part of the human experience is the desire to not feel alone when going through a troublesome situation. And yes, we are to always know that the LORD is always present, but He has also given us people to walk with us through wearisome times. Truth is often being aware of our need of not being in isolation, but it's tough to be there for others when you have so many things that are personally weighing down on you. We saw fatigue as the weight that kept Peter, James, and John from praying for Christ. We have to challenge ourselves past our own circumstance to be there for others. It's hard, but it's not impossible, especially when we rely on the Spirit for our need.

Christ's example of holding fast to the Father in the midst of this situation is inspiring, because we noted that He had just come from dedicated prayer for Himself, His disciples, and all who believe in Him. He needed the strength from the prayer that He had just finished praying. It's amazing how we'll pray for something we know we should; when what we prayed for happens, it still feels unexpected to us. This is because many times, we pray without the faith that Christ taught is the standard for prayer to the Father. Many times, our prayer comes out of procedure and not really a solemn ingestion of the moment at hand. Even worse than this is the weakness we feel when we refuse Spirit-prompted prayers. He's indicating to us that something is coming that we need to be spiritually prepared for, but we won't prepare.

When we think this through, it makes absolutely no sense, but in the moment, it makes our flesh feel good. We get to enjoy a natural comfort in place of the discipline that we need at that time. Let's challenge ourselves to really press in and give ourselves over to the Spirit's leading us to prayer at a time when we normally wouldn't be praying. Christ left a perfect example of the Father's will being done through Him that is essential for us to model our lives around. Let's be obedient.

MATTHEW WATSON

Survey

Do you have isolated times of prayer? Are you afraid of praying because you don't feel the nearness of GOD as Father? Do you want the will of the Father to be done, over and above your own will?

Supplication

Confess not devoting yourself to prayer how you should, desiring your will above the Father's will for you, and not casting your cares upon the one able to do something about them.

Commit to submitting to the Father's will, being more intentional in prayer, asking directly for what you need, and to communicating to the LORD the trouble you experience and trusting Him with the results each time.

Solicitation

Examining the life of Christ is breathtaking. It truly is remarkable to read of His life and words. Even greater than this, it is encouraging to the soul to keep going when you have such a clear and consistent example to follow when you don't know what to do. He's left for us instruction that is entirely flawless. We have the responsibility of leaning not upon our own understanding but trusting the LORD's directing our lives by way of His Spirit.

All of Me

When you have counted the costs and have made up your mind to follow after Christ and His teaching, there is but one last requirement—commitment, faithfulness, fidelity. As a believer, you must continuously choose daily to follow after Christ, as you rebel against the urgings of the world around you, Satan, and your own improper desires.

Your submission to GOD's will is the forever call upon your life. You must continue to trust yourself and your own way less, all the while continuing to trust more and more daily in the Spirit of GOD that now resides within you. This is what it means to trust and give YAH all of you.

I submit everything to my gracious and loving Master—I will settle for nothing less.

He who loves father or mother more than Me is not worthy of Me; and he who loves son or daughter more than Me is not worthy of Me. And he who does not take his cross and follow after Me is not worthy of Me. He who has found his life will lose it, and he who has lost his life for My sake will find it.

Matthew 10:37–39, NASB

"What shall we say?
'Continue in sin,
All for grace?'
We run away,
Then come back to play
In this masquerade."

Lyrics have been taken from the song, *All of Me* by Janette … ikz (Track 3, *Not My Own* EP)

Study

This passage is written following the Pharisees' condemnation of Christ. They were directly stating that He casts out demons by the ruler of demons. But in contrast to their foolishness, Christ still travels around through all of the cities and villages, working the works for which He was sent and proclaiming the Gospel of the Kingdom. He felt compassion for the crowds He would minister to because they were not a people, taken advantage of, and without a shepherd to lead them. So Christ tells His disciples that there were too few workers for the abundant harvest and they needed to cry out to the LORD of the harvest to send more workers. Immediately after this occasion, Matthew records that the twelve were then sent out. But before they were sent out, Christ had specific instruction that He wanted to convey to His disciples that they wouldn't get discouraged as they went into the harvest to labor. But the words that He shares with them would've been tremendously difficult to receive.

He states to His disciples that family relationships are not supposed to receive priority over Him, for the one who doesn't prioritize Him above all else isn't worthy of Him.

He follows this proclamation with the continued thought that the one who does not take up his cross and follow after Him is also unworthy of Him. This is the one who is unwilling to lay his or her entire life on the line for the sake of cherishing Christ above all.

Lastly, Christ finishes this picture by tying together all that He has stated, as He says that finding your life will require you to lose it and those who lose their life on His behalf will find it.

He's teaching His disciples as He's sending them out that it is going to be a tough road before them, and it's going to require every ounce of faithfulness to stay the course. His promise to them is a life worth far more than the one that they gave up on His behalf. This is because the life they sacrifice on His behalf is temporal in nature, while the one He exchanges it for is eternal.

Significance

Truly, these are hard words from our Messiah, and it takes diligence and humility to properly mine them. Often His hard terms are misunderstood as we seek to understand them outside of the context in which they were originally delivered, or we don't seek Him as we attempt to understand what it is that He is teaching. He tells us that all we need to do is ask for understanding, but we still choose not to. He wrote it and gave us His Spirit to live within us that we might understand it and live it, but we choose our own way and lean upon our own lack of understanding.

Christ is teaching here that if He is not prioritized as supreme, then He is not worthy in that person's viewpoint. For that person can only see the things that they currently have or are pursuing as their goal(s). In their mind, it would never make sense to change ambitions, since they've imagined and had their own aspirations in mind for an amount of time, and it just cannot make sense to them to abandon them for the sake of Christ. Many times, our view of Christ can be just like this. We want Him, for sure, but we cannot seem to part with the other things that we love more than Him. So we have a competition, and the competition continues until there isn't one any longer, because we have given ourselves over to Christ. As a result of this, we are able see Christ from a proper perspective, whereas this was impossible before.

Not only is this viewpoint true, but the inverse of the previous viewpoint is also correct. Christ is indicating that the person who doesn't esteem Him as worthy is not worthy of Him. In other words, there is no other way to come to Him except He be high and lifted up. For when someone truly understands the Gospel, Christ is more treasured than all else, and we can say like Asaph, "Whom have I in heaven *but You?* And besides You, I desire nothing on earth. My flesh and my heart may fail, but GOD is the strength of my heart and my portion forever." (Psalm 73:25, 26 NASB)

But the sad reality is that we are willing to prioritize a human mate who will fail us, but we are hesitant to choose the Messiah who will never and can never fail us or make a mistake. He's more worthy than any human partner we could ever choose. But many of us make partner selection the defining moment of our lives, when there is a decision that must weigh far greater on our minds. This decision is the willingness to lose our life for the sake of finding Christ.

Survey

Are you willing to prioritize Christ above all else? Are you willing to sacrifice everything to choose Christ and follow after Him? What are the things that you are currently known for and identified by? Are you willing to lay these to the side to know Christ?

Supplication

Confess loving Christ's creation more than Him, not following after Christ, and not esteeming Christ as worthy.

Commit to prioritizing Christ as the prize, to taking up you cross and following after Christ, and to finding your identity in Christ.

Solicitation

The LORD wants every part of us. The responsibility that we have is to give it. This is truly one of those things that is easier said than done, since none of us can perfectly give all of ourselves until we are glorified. The truth of desire should still remain when we ask ourselves the question, "Do I desire to give all of myself?" Christ has stated that we must count the costs. And when we do, we find Him masterfully fulfilling places we thought could never be healed or whole. Oh, taste and see that the LORD is good!

Then He said to His disciples, "If anyone wishes to come after Me, he must deny himself, and take up his cross and follow Me. For whoever wishes to save his life will lose it; but whoever loses his life for My sake will find it. For what will it profit a man if he gains the whole world and forfeits his soul? Or what will a man give in exchange for his soul?"

Matthew 16:24–26, NASB

"Every day these bodies decay
A little more,
For what team do you play?
We can be free, no longer enslaved,
Escape from these chains."

Lyrics have been taken from the song, *All of Me* by Janette … ikz (Track 3, *Not My Own* EP)

Study

We come back into Matthew's account right after Peter reveals, "You are the Christ, the Son of the living God." Christ shares with Peter that man could never reveal this truth to him, which is what makes him blessed. Right after this admission, Matthew's gospel states, "From that time …" Christ was preparing them for His suffering and imminent death. Christ begins to teach His disciples that they too must suffer on account of Him. Peter, who was just commended a few verses prior, was now being rebuked for wanting to keep the Messiah from the death He was warning them would indeed come. This leads us directly into Christ's words to His disciples in verse twenty-four.

There He states, "If anyone wishes to come after Me, he must deny himself, and take up his cross (daily) and follow Me." Christ is teaching His disciples that the life of a genuine follower of His is marked by a consistent pattern of life that denies self and preeminently places God's will at the fore. Christ then details the extent of this self-denial when He states that a cross must be borne. This accepted cross indicates that submission to Christ, even if it should mean to the point of death, is the final burden for His genuine follower.

Christ then goes on to state with even more specificity that the one who seeks to deliver/rescue/save self will actually end up losing what he or she is trying to preserve—self. But the one who faces the loss of everything or even loses everything for the namesake and the glory of God actually acquires. So the formula that Christ spells out is

$$\text{save} \times \text{self} = \text{lose} :: \text{lose} \times \text{self} = \text{gain}$$

This paradox continues as the LORD explains in greater detail what He is speaking. He states that no one profits eternally on the basis of the possession of material items on earth; and in like manner, a man's soul can be exchanged for no "thing." There's nothing for which he may swap the eternal consequences that he has labored for while here on earth.

Significance

It's incredibly easy to be a Christian in the Western world—America. I say this tongue in cheek, but it should get your attention. Because in many ways we've changed what it means to be a follower of Christ here. We've made it into something altogether different. For the most part, we don't want to consider all of Christ's words. As is the human issue, we like what we like, and we don't like what we don't. So as soon as it is convenient for us, we will ditch an aspect of something that we've come to know as truth from GOD's Word. This also shows itself as we will intentionally not take in large doses of the Word of GOD, in fear that we will be laid bare before Him. But this is not the self-denial that we have been called to walk in. We have been called to abandon our comfort for Christ to get the glory from our lives. But from both the liberal and conservative theological frameworks, we're sold Christian comfort, just packaged differently.

The prosperity formula teaches that Christ is at your beck and call and you command material things from Him because He owes you. Your material prosperity is what His suffering and crucifixion were all about. This is false. This is heretical.
The conservative packaging is wrapped in Bible language about gathering and hoarding resources for all of your future

generations to come. Once you have amassed enough wealth for your children, you then progress to your grandchildren; after them you move to your great-grandchildren, etc. But this is just as false and heretical as well. In both of these views, an excessive amount of wealth is kept for self, whereas self could've been denied for the sake of Christ being honored more in this world. In my short stay here on this earth, I've been fortunate to meet believers who challenge themselves to look at their finances the way that scripture challenges us to. They not only give toward global Christian advancement but also to the underdeveloped sections of their city or town and those doing the hard work there.

When you look at them, you would never know what they make because they don't buy fancy things. They truly want to be able to give anything they have, should there be a request or need. This is self-denial, but the truth is that we don't want the challenge that this Christianity presents to us. Here in the United States, we will shout that we will die for the sake of the Gospel, while daily refusing to live in accordance with this same Gospel. It is easy to proclaim an allegiance when the threat of harm isn't real.

What is Christ's message for us? Do not live for material things, because they can never provide for you what you are seeking from them. You'll buy and acquire, only to realize that the more you purchase, the more the desire to purchase grows. The very fact that Christ speaks about the inability of man to preserve his own life should be firmly noted, as that is exactly what we seek to do when we make purchases. It is this very pursuit of things that causes for the one seeking to lose his life. For things and the attaining of them become his focus. But Christ wants every follower of His to know that you cannot take anything with you when you leave this earth. No matter how many things you accrue while on this earth, none of it will help you to enter into His dwelling place for all of eternity.

Survey

Do you regularly deny yourself? Is it your habit to do what you want when you want? Are you aware of what Christ is calling you to give up right now?

Supplication

Confess your selfishness, lack of self-denial, and not putting Christ first.

Commit to denying self, not loving the things of this world, not desiring after material things, and to desiring the will of GOD above all else.

Solicitation

Christ teaches His disciples that He is to be first in all things. Specifically, He teaches them that for Him to be first in their lives, they must deny themselves. Anyone unwilling to deny self doesn't truly belong to Him. But what is the line? If a purchase is sinful for one person and not the next, how then can we really know? We know by asking the LORD to examine our hearts. Because each one's heart is naturally sinful and untrustworthy, we cannot trust ourselves with the litmus test of our self-denial. We have to trust that work to the Spirit of GOD living within us.

But Jesus said to him, "No one, after putting his hand to the plow and looking back, is fit for the kingdom of God."

Luke 9:62, NASB

"Disobeyed,
Still He came
Left the throne,
Took my place,
Wretched I am
Lion and Lamb—
The Son of man!
Oh! What manner of love!"

Lyrics have been taken from the song, *All of Me* by Janette … ikz (Track 3, *Not My Own* EP)

Study

Leading up to Christ's teaching His disciples about the testing of faithfulness to Him, His disciples had the opportunity to experience some amazing occurrences. These events sparked their zeal, but Christ knew that it was necessary to temper their experiences together with Him through hard truth. So this is exactly what He does; He gives them heavy doses of truth that they are ill-prepared to receive.

The disciples observe firsthand miracles that shake them to the core. The miracles cause them to perceive Him afresh, while asking among themselves who He is. They understood with veiled view His greatness but were unable to attain the level of His majesty.

Christ wanted them to understand that working under His authority had costs that they needed to weigh and understand. "I will follow you" is repeated to Him multiple times, but Christ meets it with a tolerant correction. He wants them to understand that sacrifice will be necessary in order to be pleasing to Him in doing His work.

With the disciples, Christ is pointing out to them that nothing can be more important than doing the work that you have been entrusted to accomplish. Christ is teaching them a concept that we already had the privilege of looking into, which is the idea of worthiness. For one continuously looking back, after setting his hand upon the plow, proves to be unworthy. Christ is teaching them that in order for them to truly follow Him, they would need to understand Him as the everlasting leader in the kingdom of God.

Significance

Christ goes into great detail the cost of being His disciple, because the disciples were gathering an improper picture of what it meant. His disciples were taking the things that they liked and appreciated about being a disciple and seeking to build upon those things all while neglecting the focus that Christ was teaching them that they must have. Examples of this can be seen in Christ challenging their lack of faith and in their inability to perform miracles they had been sent out to accomplish. Christ understood the thoughts given to Him as excuses, but we often call these reasons. Granted, we don't have the Messiah walking around, but His requirement is still the same. He requires that we aren't misguided in our working the harvest. For if our hand is to the plow, but we are unceasingly looking backward, then it will be impossible to accomplish the goals He entrusts to us for His kingdom. In looking backward, we are completely unaware of our ineffectiveness for the kingdom.

The LORD calls the one seeking to work on His behalf in this way unfit/unusable. This is exactly what He means; this individual is useless for the kingdom. It takes incredible intentionality to present the Gospel to an individual, and the who one continuously finds reason not to is incapable of doing what Christ requires.

But what if, in seeking to take the sting away from words that Christ really used in His cultural context, we miss the point? Saying that someone is worthless is a hard statement. But as believers of Christ and His words, would we dare distrust their accuracy? Seasonal doubt is a normal part of the Christian experience, but if you decide to distrust the very words of Christ, then in whose words will you trust in their place?

Many times our proclamation of Christ falls short of understanding Christ's very own words. We look around and try to uncover others and their lack of Gospel faithfulness, but if we're honest, we don't spend the same amount or nearly enough effort on seeking to unearth our own unfaithfulness. Exploring our own hypocrisies is the Christian's work. We must first take this work seriously if we want to take the LORD's work seriously.

Survey

Are you committed to following Christ? What does your commitment to following Him look like? What have you had to let go of for the sake of being faithful to the proclamation of the Gospel? Would you classify your life as one that is fit for Gospel proclamation?

Supplication

Confess your lack of faithfulness to your Gospel calling.

Commit to remaining faithful to the Gospel work to which you have been called and to not allowing anything to get in the way of faithfully serving Christ.

Solicitation

This text presents to us the reality that we must critically assess our own Gospel faithfulness. We must ask ourselves if we are living as faithfully as we know how; if we are, then examining ourselves to learn more to live more faithfully. Christ has already warned that the one who doesn't live intentionally working on His behalf is not fit for His kingdom. We can prove ourselves fit as we rely on His Spirit to work the work that He has allotted each of us.

"So then, none of you can be My disciple who does not give up all his own possessions. Therefore, salt is good; but if even salt has become tasteless, with what will it be seasoned? It is useless either for the soil or for the manure pile; it is thrown out. He who has ears to hear, let him hear."

Luke 14:33-35, NASB

"What do you see,
When you're looking at me?
Are you even pleased?
That's all that matters to me."

Lyrics have been taken from the song, *All of Me* by Janette ... ikz (Track 3, *Not My Own* EP)

Study

These verses come as Christ's popularity with the people is steadily rising, while the Pharisees' resentment toward Him grows in like manner—they were watching Him very closely. He shares with the Pharisees, at a dinner He was invited to, words that indict them. He also heals a man on the Sabbath at this same time, but in the moment, no one vocally takes issue with it when He asks and proceeds to do it.

He leaves this Pharisee's home, and the crowds that are following Him continue to travel with Him. After hearing all about Him and His miracles, including the one most recently recorded, surely there were some additional members who would have begun to travel as well. He knew it was the right time to continue to teach what it really meant to follow Him, in contrast to simply following Him in hopes to see and be a part of what would happen next.

Christ begins with a familiar teaching of His, that He had taught before about the need for sacrificing to be a disciple of His. He exalts Himself over all human relationships and even the individual's own life. Christ teaches His familiar teaching as an individual carrying their cross. The cross was synonymous with sacrificing oneself, even to the point of death, which was Christ's own mission.

Christ takes this idea and builds upon it sideways as He likens what He has said to a builder beginning to build without counting the costs for the building that he is constructing. Christ identifies this one as receiving ridicule, since he didn't know that he would be unable to finish what he had begun, as a result of a lack of resources.

He complements His presentation as He presents an example of a king setting out for battle and counting the costs of this potential battle. Christ's point is that any reasonable king would consider whether he is able to win a battle before deciding to engage in one. He states that there will be a request for peace if the king believes he is unable to win the battle.

After building sideways in His last two examples, Christ now decides to build upon His original statement. He reiterates by teaching that His disciples must be willing to turn away from any- and everything for the sake of following after Him. Christ was to have no equal to His Lordship. So when He makes the comparison of discipleship with salt, He's teaching them that there is no middle ground. Either an individual is with Christ wholeheartedly or he isn't; the indication is found in not allowing anything to come before Him.

Significance

As a Christian culture, we must ask ourselves are we producing genuine disciples of Christ or followers of something entirely different. This question is one that should be ever embedded in the forefront of our minds as we seek to live out Gospel fidelity. We don't have the freedom to ignore this reality of false conversion, because the result is eternal. Christ understood the necessity of saying things that would cause some to discontinue following after Him. If this was true for Him, why would we think that it would be any easier for us in our fallen condition. We have a natural tendency to sway and veer from the truth, but this wasn't so for Christ.

We see from Him that no one else on earth could require what He has required. Being who He is, He must require all the allegiance that He has required. The main message of our presentation isn't often telling individuals that they must count the cost before pledging commitment to Christ. People need to know that the journey is going to be rough, but that the LORD has always been faithful. When the message isn't introduced in this way, it often leads to resentment and discontentment because of failed expectations.

After making the decision to follow after Christ, we must understand that the goal is to not let anything get in the way of this daily-renewed decision. This is what Christ is explaining when He speaks of hatred, cross carrying, and giving up all of your possessions. For we also end up seeing the compassion that Christ feels later on in His conversation with the rich young ruler. Giving up all of his belongings would never save him, but these things did get in the way of his pledging allegiance to Christ. We must never allow anything to get in the way of our commitment.

Survey

Are you willing to not allow anything to get in between you and your relationship with Christ? Have you decided that you are willing to sacrifice even your life for the sake of Christ? Have you counted the costs of what it's going to take from you to make this journey with the LORD?

Supplication

Confess allowing yourself to be separated from Christ and to loving this world and the fleeting items it offers.

Commit to carrying your cross, to not allowing anything to separate you from your love of Christ, and to praying for wisdom for the journey ahead.

Solicitation

It's not unreasonable for Christ to require that His disciples be willing to experience what He endured. He's the only Son of the Almighty, and He had to experience the worst form of death. We have to challenge the idea of the fear of death because many times it cripples us to the point of inaction, as we experience paralysis for fear of death. But death isn't the worst thing that could happen to us; it is actually the best. Now this isn't some martyr talk, because it's safe and easy to do that in the comfort of a land without persecution; but rather, this is lot acceptance. LORD, whatever you want to do in my life, I commit to not intentionally getting in your way to attempt to frustrate your plan for me.

Now He was also saying to the disciples, "There was a rich man who had a manager, and this *manager* was reported to him as squandering his possessions. And he called him and said to him, 'What is this I hear about you? Give an accounting of your management, for you can no longer be manager.' The manager said to himself, 'What shall I do, since my master is taking the management away from me? I am not strong enough to dig; I am ashamed to beg. I know what I shall *do*, so that when I am removed from the management people will welcome me into their homes.' And he summoned each one of his master's debtors, and he *began* saying to the first, 'How much do you owe my master?' And he said, 'A hundred measures of oil.' And he said to him, 'Take your bill, and sit down quickly and write fifty.' Then he said to another, 'And how much do you owe?' And he said, 'A hundred measures of wheat.' He said to him, 'Take your bill, and write eighty.' And his master praised the unrighteous manager because he had acted shrewdly; for the sons of this age are more shrewd in relation to their own kind than the sons of light. And I say to you, make friends for yourselves by means of the wealth of unrighteousness, so that when it fails, they will receive you into the eternal dwellings."

Luke 16:1–9, NASB (part 1 of 2)

"Wanna try a different way.
Wanna go a different pace.
All the things I'm thinking that I wanted,
'Til I met His endless love and grace."

Lyrics have been taken from the song, *All of Me* by Janette … ikz (Track 3, *Not My Own* EP)

Study

Christ continues His teaching, and as He does, He begins to speak directly to His disciples. There is no indication that the tax collectors and the sinners have departed from Him, and we know that the Pharisees are present because they show their continual displeasure with His teaching.

In disregard of the Pharisees' approval, Christ begins His next parable, picking up on the same theme as His last, wastefulness of possessions.

Christ begins this parable introducing a rich man and his manager who was not managing but was wasteful. What's going on is reported to the rich man, and he lets his manager know that he will no longer be his manager and that he needs to give an account for his management. When presented with this reality, the manager begins to think of other possibilities of work he could perform. After failing to think of work, he decides that he will devise a plan that will place him in good favor with his master's debtors, so that they would welcome him when he is without work.

He begins to summon each one who owed his master and had them lower the amount that they owed. Christ gives us two examples of his doing this. Christ states next that the master praises the manager for his shrewdness in the face of his coming struggle. The master praises the manager for this foresight to look out for himself.

Christ goes on to teach his disciples to make friends for themselves by means of the money/possessions of this earth. They were not to attach themselves to it, for the mission they were on was an eternal one, and their resources were to be used for that purpose. Christ assures them that if they do this, they will be received into heaven when they have finished their course.

Significance

Material possessions and money will never solve the eternal problems of the soul. Those who have spent most of their lives without abundance seem to think that as soon as they get this world's goods, everything will change for them. All the while, those who were born with it understand that things aren't the most important, because they still face a lot of the exact same problems that plague all humans. For these problems common to humans can never be solved by spending. So never place your faith and hope in the material, because it comes to an end at some point.

Christ teaches us that we are to use our resources to make friends for ourselves here in our stay on earth. What should be understood is that these are individuals we have developed a connection with and a deep regard for. This relationship was built upon our sharing the message of salvation along with our resources. This is the way we are to use our resources, for we understand that the material things that we acquire can never eternally travel with us. Those we have befriended by way of our evangelism and discipleship will be in heaven with us because of the LORD's graciousness upon our human efforts.

Survey

Are you willing to give up you resources for the sake of the Gospel? Are you willing to exercise shrewdness for the purpose of people coming to know the Lord in a saving way? Do you see eternity with Christ as the most important end?

Supplication

Confess not thinking eternally with your resources and acting irresponsibly with resources.

Commit to understanding in greater detail the responsibility that you have for your resources and to acting responsibly as you think eternally about the resources that you have been entrusted to manage.

Solicitation

We must be mindful of the truth that Christ has not called us to acquire resources in an unrighteous way; nor has He commended shrewdness attached to unrighteousness. He has called us to be sons of light and not get entangled in the sneaky ways that this world operates. It may seem like a good opportunity in the moment, but never think that needing a little time to pray about it will keep you from something that the Lord wants you to have, because this will never be the case. He wants us to come to Him in all things. Don't simply rush in; take your time in decision-making. You will always be satisfied knowing that you are taking your next step with your Father's approval.

"He who is faithful in a very little thing is faithful also in much; and he who is unrighteous in a very little thing is unrighteous also in much. Therefore if you have not been faithful in the *use of* unrighteous wealth, who will entrust the true *riches* to you? And if you have not been faithful in *the use of* that which is another's, who will give you that which is your own? No servant can serve two masters; for either he will hate the one and love the other, or else he will be devoted to one and despise the other. You cannot serve GOD and wealth."

Luke 16:10-13, NASB (part 2 of 2)

"King on the Cross,
Blood shed for me
All that I have is this life that You gave and it's Yours (Yours, Yours)."

Lyrics have been taken from the song, *All of Me* by Janette … ikz (Track 3, *Not My Own* EP)

Study

After concluding the parable, Christ continues His synopsis of what He is teaching His disciples. Continuing on the idea of properly managing resources and possessions, He now switches gears to teach them principles of fidelity that they are to live by.

He teaches them that faithfulness in smaller matters grows trust to the point that they may then be trusted with larger matters. He follows this by specifying that the same is true for unrighteousness. Those who are unrighteous when responsible over a smaller amount will also be act in an unrighteous way in larger matters also.

Christ then connects this teaching to the topic of possessions and wealth, which is the same topic He has been speaking about for the entire time. He then asks if a person is unfaithful with the money and possessions that have passed through their hands here on this earth, then who will entrust him with the most valuable eternal riches? The rhetorical answer here is that no one would realistically trust this one's faithfulness over eternal things when he couldn't properly manage the temporary things with which he was entrusted.

Christ then takes this same idea and paints a clear picture parallel to the one He has already illustrated. He asks here if a person is unfaithful with that which belonged to another, who would give him his own to squander? This rhetorical question also receives the clear answer that no one would responsibly do this. A reasonable person wouldn't give resources to an individual who improperly manages the resources of someone else.

Christ finishes the parable by giving a principle that is the driving force of this entire section of teaching. There cannot be two masters; there can only be one. He's letting them know that their actions will show the allegiance to be toward one over the other. Christ is teaching them there doesn't need to be this battle within them about service to Him or service to themselves with loving resources. He's commanding them to choose to love Him.

Significance

Christ requires faithfulness. He demands that His disciples are faithful to Him and His commands. Christ spells out in this parable that we have a responsibility to be faithful in even the smallest of matters. We can't think to ourselves or seek to convince ourselves that it doesn't matter, because it does. Christ said if you're faithful over very small matters, then you will be faithful in larger matters.

Many times, we want to be trusted by the Lord with more, but we refuse to be faithful over what we have already been entrusted with. We have to train ourselves to live faithfully in all matters.

When we look back at the parable that Christ created to teach His disciples, we see that the manager was unfaithful over his master's resources. This unfaithfulness led to his unrighteous action in stealing from his master by forging debtors' notes that were owed to his master. Thus he proves himself unable to be trusted with anything of his own, since he acted unfaithfully with his master's resources. The problem with the manager was that he was seeking to serve both his master and himself with his master's resources that he had complete access to. What he was attempting is impossible, and that is Christ's point.

But how many times do we seek to serve Christ and resources? We try to straddle the fence as if it is possible, but we are well aware that it isn't. We need to steady our devotion to the LORD and make sure we see resources as what they are meant to be by His definition. If we don't, we place ourselves at risk for creating an idol to displace the LORD in our lives.

Survey

Are you known for your faithfulness? Do you look for shortcuts in your responsibilities? Do you have a tendency toward loving money and material things? How do you protect yourself from loving things more than the LORD?

Supplication

Confess your lack of faithfulness in responsibilities, loving money and material things, and being divided in your love for the LORD.

Commit to faithfulness to the LORD, to faithfulness in all matters (even the ones considered small), and to being devoted to the LORD.

Solicitation

Fidelity is a character trait that isn't greatly praised as it was in decades and centuries past. Even a fake or false sense of faithfulness in engagements isn't sought out anymore from the majority culture. What are we to do with this change? I'll tell you what we are *not* to do, and that is to follow it. Christ is specific here as He speaks about faithfulness and not being divided in our devotion toward Him. Let's seek to be obedient and quickly confess our disobedience when we come up short. That's what He wants! He wants us to act responsibly and understand our accountability toward Him. If we are consistently focused on improving with these areas, He will be pleased.

Mahogany Pain

It is truly important that we daily continue to give ourselves over to the Lord, for in Him we have safety from life's storms. Not that we will be kept *from* them; rather we are kept *in* them. It's as we are continuously preserved that we grow in our trust of the Lord, and from this trust, we cry out, "Have thine own way." Growth in Christ is being able to forsake your own self-interest as you run with passion toward YAH.

The encouragement we get from the Word is that we are to suffer well, in like manner with our Lord, and receive the glory that awaits us after this life is over. And the glory of being with our Savior and Lord forevermore is to far outweigh the suffering that we experience in this short stay here on earth.

My Master knows what's best for me, so I will trust Him instead of trusting in myself, especially when I don't understand what He is doing.

And not only this, but we also exult in our tribulations, knowing that tribulation brings about perseverance; and perseverance, proven character; and proven character, hope; and hope does not disappoint, because the love of God has been poured out within our hearts through the Holy Spirit who was given to us.

Romans 5:3-5, NASB

"Please, don't take this pain away.
Somehow, I feel,
It's for my own good."

Lyrics have been taken from the song, *Mahogany Pain* by Janette … ikz (Track 4, *Not My Own* EP)

Study

Paul is writing to the believers in Rome, laying out the doctrine that they were to adhere to. He has just finished explaining to them the faith that they have and the initial source of that faith. Now he is going to take some time to explain to them what it means to have this faith and what they should expect in their lives as a result of the aforementioned faith. Paul explains to them that the grace the believer experiences is to result in praise; not just a praise for the introduction, but also for the future hope that has been promised them. There then comes a swift transition as Paul uses the same terminology to describe how these believers were to respond in times of adversity.

Paul lets them know in verse 3 that they were to praise in the midst of their experienced tribulations. Paul's point was that this would increase the ability within them to endure and to bear. He then teaches that in their bearing up and enduring, they would be giving proof and evidence to the faith that is within them. Paul closes his argument in the exact same place that he began—hope. This hope comes as a result of the evidence from their bearing up under trials.

Paul goes on to explain that this hope will never disappoint, because God's love has been poured out upon them through the Holy Spirit, and this is their assurance. They can have full faith in their hope because it is completely based upon evidence within their daily reality.

Significance

It is counterintuitive to praise in the midst of experiencing tribulation, but this is exactly what Paul is describing. We have the responsibility to exalt in tribulations. We must understand that we are able to do this because the LORD's goodness isn't contingent upon the circumstance in which we find ourselves, whether good or bad. It is in this place that we are truly able to learn how to endure. The lessons learned aren't false, but we really learn how to learn and depend upon Christ in trying circumstances.

Much of our strength for this faith journey can be found in the time spent on this journey. No, there aren't any points that we naturally get for being accepted by Christ for a certain period of time, but there is a strengthening and proving of genuineness of faith after having the LORD bring you through many situations. We begin to know Him in ways that we once only knew *about* Him. As this evidence builds, we grow closer and closer to Him as we learn to trust Him more.

It is as we learn to trust Christ more that our hope becomes more and more real. It becomes more real because as we see the continual evidence of the Spirit's work in our lives, we know that He will complete this work He is doing within us. This is where our initial praise may be found—hoping in the glory that is to come, which far outweighs any of the trouble we have experienced in our stay on earth.

Survey

Do you see the trials of your personal life as a reason to sin or complain? Do you find it easy to give up when you are being pressed? Are you aware of the Spirit's presence within you when you struggle? What does your hope look like on a day-to-day basis?

Supplication

Confess not praising the LORD in the midst of your trials, not enduring in the midst of your situation, and not hoping in your future reality of being made like Christ.

Commit to trusting in the LORD in the midst of adverse times and to trusting in the evidence that the LORD gives you to confirm that He is with you and hasn't gone anywhere.

Solicitation

It's easy to say to someone, "Trust GOD." It's an entirely different world for each one to trust Christ in the way that He is causing for you to need to. For many times we seek to judge others' struggles, for they are often far different from our current ones. But what if instead of judging others' struggles we actually reached out to offer the same help that was given to us by the Spirit? This would be a game changer, and a lot of believers' lives would be changed, because our first inclination when we see someone struggle is to help if we can. We have a responsibility to praise the LORD in the midst of our tribulations, but sometimes that praise comes easier with a hand to hold. Will you be that hand of grace for another in the faith and allow yourself to receive it as well?

The Spirit Himself testifies with our spirit that we are children of God, and if children, heirs also, heirs of God and fellow heirs with Christ, if indeed we suffer with *Him* so that we may also be glorified with *Him*. For I consider that the sufferings of this present time are not worthy to be compared with the glory that is to be revealed to us.

Romans 8:16-18, NASB

"And all I know
Is this weary soul longs to see You,
On that day!"

Lyrics have been taken from the song, *Mahogany Pain* by Janette … ikz (Track 4, *Not My Own* EP)

Study

Paul continues to explain more deeply these believers' understanding of the relationship with the God that they have. He's teaching them how they should stand in the midst of knowledge that they possess. They should be more encouraged to stand firmly in the midst of their suffering, since they know it has a purpose.

Paul teaches them that the Spirit agrees with their spirit about their relationship with the LORD. In other words, the Spirit informs their spirit that they are children of God. They understood this in connection with their relationship with Christ.

They understood that they would receive glory in like manner with the Messiah, since He was the only Son of God. Christ being the promised heir of God, His siblings (believers) could state this same claim of being heir alongside Christ.

Paul explains to them that they couldn't be co-heirs of benefit only; they must be co-heirs in every way that Christ would individually require them to be. Paul's connection for them was that if they were to suffer with Him, they would be glorified with Him in the end.

Paul encouraged them in view of this truth that no matter the suffering they would experience, it could never compare with the glory that would be revealed in them. This was to be the founding truth upon which their lives rested.

Significance

Ever feel like something was too good to be true? Oftentimes when we feel that way, it is because what we are experiencing truly is. Sooner than later, we frequently find out that there's a catch! But when we come to the Word of GOD, we have to allow for this idea to fade as we learn about the person GOD is and discover more of His character. Not only is He perfect, but everything that He does and the way that He does it is perfect also. Selah.

He knows that our lives need a healthy balance of good and bad, for if our lives were to lean too heavily to one side over another, we would be ready to call it quits. But in His perfection, He knows exactly what we need and exactly when we need it. What Paul is teaching us here is that suffering is a part of our adoption. Not that we need to receive some sort of punishment or initiation to be a part of the family, but that it's a part of everyone in the family's journey—including the Messiah.

Christ couldn't avoid suffering during His time on earth, and He is GOD in the flesh. If we are prone to sin, wander, exalt ourselves, etc., don't you think it is necessary to keep all of these things in check by allowing situations to occur where we realize our sense of need with a heightened awareness? There are certain lessons that He knows we will only learn through hardship and struggle. We've already made the decision to trust Him for what comes after this life; the next step is to trust Him for whatever may come in this one.

MATTHEW WATSON

Survey

How do you know that you are a child of GOD? Do you have a proper view of Christian suffering, or do you believe that Christians only suffer because of sin in their lives? When you suffer, what do you find your mind to be focused upon?

Supplication

Confess not viewing suffering with Christ properly and not being focused upon Christ and His eternal promises.

Commit to suffering with eternity on your mind and to trusting that the LORD knows perfectly.

Solicitation

The LORD has initiated and authenticated our relationship with Him. He has taken His Spirit and placed Him on the inside of us and this Spirit that He has given us encourages us in the middle of the fight. It may appear as though we have lost, but He encourages us from within that ultimately we will win. His encouragement gives us the strength that we need to fight another day. He encourages us toward the example of our Christ, and we know that everything is worth it. The end result is going to far surpass that which our minds are even able comprehend before the glorification that is to come. So in this way, just trust that all that He has said is true because all that He has said has been true.

For momentary, light affliction is producing for us an eternal weight of glory far beyond all comparison, while we look not at the things which are seen, but at the things which are not seen; for the things which are seen are temporal, but the things which are not seen are eternal.

2 Corinthians 4:17–18, NASB

"If loving You in the storm
Is when I love You the most,
Then rain on me forever!"

Lyrics have been taken from the song, *Mahogany Pain* by Janette … ikz (Track 4, *Not My Own* EP)

Study

In order to properly understand the exhortation that Paul provides for the Corinthian believers, we must first recap a few things he has already stated a little earlier in this letter.

Back in verses 7-10, Paul lays out his plight of suffering as a believer and he wants the Corinthian believers to know that they too will suffer; but they were not to allow the suffering they experienced to consume them. They instead were to focus in the great glory the LORD would receive through them in their obedience.

Paul admonishes the Corinthian believers in this passage not to lose sight of the purpose of suffering; and to help them, he reminded them of the Messiah's revelation to them and their consequent turn from their sin. After this explanation, he went on to detail to them their involvement and the purpose for their experience.

Paul describes his Christian experience in such a way that doesn't truly make sense to those outside of the faith. He describes having trouble in every way, but he isn't cornered with the inability to move by these hardships. He further describes living with uncertainty, doubt, and anxiety about what is going to be but not giving up. Paul then describes being harassed but cared for in the midst of the trouble. Lastly, he finishes his series of analogies with greatly suffering and badly hurting but not perishing or coming to ruin.

Paul's point in extensively describing all of this is that he wanted the Corinthian believers to understand the purpose for his suffering. He wanted them to be fully aware that they too would suffer and their suffering was to be best understood as being directly linked to Christ's affliction on their behalf.

With this as Paul's context of presentation, he explains himself further through another series of contrast in verses 17 and 18 that he wanted the Corinthians to understand. He begins with his contrast of the momentary and comparatively limited nature of their affliction with the eternal and incomprehensibly valuable glory that it would produce. Paul then continues his caution to them as he reinforces to them their responsibility to that which is unseen above that which is seen, since those things that cannot be seen are eternal in significance.

Significance

It is so easy to get lost in how a culture presents the Messiah's message and what His message really was or is. Added to this is the fact that often when people reject *Him,* they often are only rejecting that presenter's version, since they weren't presented with a full or accurate picture of the Christ to make a decision based upon. The truth is when viewing the complete message from scripture, it has a power to do its own compelling and repelling. Our presentation doesn't need to seek to do either, although naturally our presentation will do both at different points.

The whole message teaches us that we will go though in this life, and it teaches us how we are to go through in being ambassadors for our King. We are to be like Paul in considering our sufferings and trouble to be momentary. The truth is that a sincere believer's troubles could endure for the entirety of his or her life. So, in human terms, to suffer for a lifetime isn't momentary. To endure suffering for a lifetime is to endure suffering and hardship for a long time. The reality that the believer is to focus in on is the eternal one that will truly matter in the end.

Along with the extent of time, the magnitude of suffering can also vary for the believer. Some believers' suffering reaches the realm of persecution and cannot be likened to anything else except persecution. Paul, having experienced a great amount of persecution, was able to say that his persecution wasn't intense. Paul, in view of eternity, said that all that he had gone through was limited in scale. This was because he had his eyes set on his eternal glorious reward.

We must take our cues from the Apostle Paul's words to the churches at Corinth. We must set our gaze upon that which is not seen, for that will last forever. We have to constantly fight against the troubles that seek to distract us from the eternal home that we have with our Lord.

Survey

Do you view Christian suffering as something you shouldn't experience? Do you find yourself able to understand, in time of trouble, that suffering is extremely limited? Are you aware of the greatness of the glory awaiting all who endure to the end? Do you find yourself to be more focused on the temporal or eternal?

Supplication

Confess not considering the troubles of this world to be fleeting and limited and to not focusing on eternity.

Commit to focusing on life with Christ and to approaching suffering through the lenses of eternity.

Solicitation

We often miss realities that exist right before us because don't desire to see them as the truth. We so badly want something else to be the truth, and we will drown ourselves in this fantasy to avoid what really is true. We must teach ourselves to build our hope on eternity and not today's distractions. We mature when our initial response to adverse circumstance is reflecting upon its nonexistence in comparison to the glory that awaits the believer.

Blessed is a man who perseveres under trial; for once he has been approved, he will receive the crown of life which *the Lord* has promised to those who love Him.

James 1:12, NASB

"Please, (please, please)
Ignore these tears overflowing with pain;
As my fists tightly grip,
Your thorns of sufficient grace."

Lyrics have been taken from the song, *Mahogany Pain* by Janette … ikz (Track 4, *Not My Own* EP)

Study

The brother of Christ has encouragement that he shares with dispersed Jewish Christians. He wants them to know that they must endure under their tests and trials to receive the LORD's promise.

James begins back in verse 2, where he instructs the Jewish Christians on how to properly engage when they are experiencing a test of their faith. He lets them know that when they are being tested in a plurality of ways, they need to consider all of the testing joyous. He told them to do this because he wanted them fully aware of the fact that this testing would produce something within them. Their faith being tried through adverse circumstances would produce endurance within them.

Their ability to bear and endure under the hardship that they were facing would result in them being what the LORD would have them to be. The LORD wanted them to be complete, whole, and presented as mature. He didn't want their faith to be lacking, since it had not been tested. It was necessary for them to experience a diversity of trials, so that they may be able to prove to themselves that their faith in Christ is genuine.

James comes back later on in verse 12 with special words for the believer who endures under the weight of personal testing. He places this believer in the category of being happy and experiencing the favor of the LORD. James states that this is true because of the eternal reward that will be received by those who endure to the end.

Significance

Testing proves authenticity. Whenever we desire to find out whether something is real and genuine, we put it to the test. This testing ranges from the quality of precious metals all of the way to seeking to verify a person's authentic affiliation with an organization. No matter the reason for the testing, we test because we don't know what the outcome will be; but when the LORD tests, it is for us to prove our own sincerity to ourselves. For He already knows everything that is in us, and our responses to testing could never catch Him by surprise.

This is why we are to count as joy our testing by way of differing trials. It's because it will truly bring the believer great joy to know that he or she is walking in obedience to the LORD, for this is the approval that they have been seeking. These believers have let go of the pursuit of humans' temporary satisfaction with them and replaced it with the LORD's ultimate satisfaction and have found it to be all they need. James understood this and taught these Jewish believers it was truly a privilege to be tested.

He is teaching them also that in understanding the privilege that they had in being tried by the LORD, it was necessary for them to respond appropriately to the trial. Because right after the verse that we have been examining, it says that no one should say that GOD is tempting an individual toward sin. He is making this distinction because that's exactly the goal of testing: it proves the nature of something. He's warning them that if they bend and give in to sin during their time of trial, they are proving what is within them.

The same warning is true for us if we don't respond appropriately within the trials the Lord provides for us to be tested in. In the same way that they were not to be deceived, we are not to be deceived in thinking that the Lord would ever lead us in the direction of sin or temptation. We know that He steers us clear of sin by way of His Word and His Spirit dwelling within us; He faithfully provides ways out of each snare of temptation in which we find ourselves trapped.

For James, to be tested is to experience the favor of the Lord and to know true happiness. This is what he wanted their hope to be in and what our hope is to be in. With our minds focused upon enduring with great joy, we must persevere that we may, in the end, be approved.

Survey

Do you find yourself trusting the Spirit of God to endure when you're being tested? Do you understand endurance during testing to be favor from God and to be rejoiced in? Do you respond to trials in a way that proves you love the Lord more than your comfort?

Supplication

Confess not viewing trials in the same way that the Lord does and not being committed to enduring the trials the Lord has provided for you.

Commit to enduring in the midst of being tested, to loving the Lord, and to living an approved life.

MATTHEW WATSON

Solicitation

We are blessed to be able to endure in the testing of our faith, for perseverance is truly a gift from the LORD. No one can boast that they were the reason they successfully passed a spiritual test they were presented. Everyone who is successful has the LORD to thank, which is why they are favored. GOD graces us with the ability to respond appropriately, but we have the responsibility to choose to not respond like the one without faith. When we respond appropriately to trials, we energize ourselves closer and closer toward the final goal—eternity with Christ.

Beloved, do not be surprised at the fiery ordeal among you, which comes upon you for your testing, as though some strange thing were happening to you; but to the degree that you share the sufferings of Christ, keep on rejoicing, so that also at the revelation of His glory you may rejoice with exultation.

1 Peter 4:12–13, NASB

"If in excruciating pain
Is when I call Your Name,
Then break these bones forever!"

Lyrics have been taken from the song, *Mahogany Pain* by Janette ... ikz (Track 4, *Not My Own* EP)

Study

Peter's first letter is one of encouragement to believers who were without a home and found themselves strangers in lands not their own. Along with their alien residency, they also found themselves greatly persecuted because of their identification with the Messiah. Peter writes to embolden them in faithfulness of service to Christ.

He tells them to not allow themselves to be filled with wonder or be shocked at the pain that they were experiencing. They were to know that pain and suffering was to be a part of their lives and commitment to Christ. But even greater than this, Peter lets them know the reasoning behind their sorrow was for their testing. He's letting them know that grief was not to be foreign or unfamiliar to them. They were to be acquainted with heartache as a result of their identification with the Messiah.

James connected a simple truth that would factor in the extent of suffering. He lets them know that no matter the amount of pain they were called to suffer, they were to understand it as a part of their imitation of Christ. As He suffered unjustly, so they must also. Peter then instructs them that they were to be continuously rejoicing in the midst of their struggle.

The reason Peter connected for these believers was that when Christ is revealed, there will be an even greater sense of jubilation. They were encouraged to rejoice in their suffering now, because their rejoicing would be tremendously greater to them when Christ returns.

Significance

Suffering is an unavoidable aspect of the Christian experience. There isn't a scale of how much suffering one must go through, but the principle is that the one who genuinely believes must suffer. To take it a step further, Peter makes it clear that we should expect suffering and not be alarmed when it comes. Peter is also warning against a believer who suffers because of their personal choice to sin. Whether the choice was made from a place of ignorance or intentionality, the truth is that this type of suffering isn't included in what's being described. Suffering on behalf of Christ is the only suffering that is in Peter's purview.

We should also be clear to point out that Peter is not glorifying self-abasement or irresponsibility. Not to have anything during your short stay on this earth doesn't make a believer more holy, in the same way as having abundance doesn't make you less holy. Peter specifically states that each one has his degree of suffering that they are to be faithful in. Though it is natural for us to do it, suffering isn't comparative. So we constantly remind ourselves that we are not to look around during our suffering for Christ, but we are to be looking upward to our motivation—the Christ. Let's rejoice and be glad at the privilege we get to share in like manner with what Christ had to endure.

Survey

Is it shocking to you when the LORD tests you? Do you view testing as something that should be unfamiliar to you? Are you willing to accept the scope of suffering that you must share with Christ? Do you rejoice in your suffering?

MATTHEW WATSON

Supplication

Confess not expecting to suffer with Christ and not accepting the extent that Christ has called you to suffer with Him.

Commit to passing every test that the LORD allows with eager expectation and focusing on the privilege of sharing with Christ in the way He sees best for you.

Solicitation

To suffer in sin or as the immediate result of sin is not what the Apostle Peter has been teaching. The only form of commendation in suffering has been within the context of suffering as a result of being a believer. This is our motivation: to suffer well and to truly be joyous in being able to suffer in like manner with the Messiah. Our rejoicing will be so much greater when Christ is revealed with all might and all power. For this is the day that we, who believe, so long for!

After you have suffered for a little while, the GOD of all grace, who called you to His eternal glory in Christ, will Himself perfect, confirm, strengthen *and* establish you.

1 Peter 5:10, NASB

"Cut it off.
Take it out.
Whatever it takes,
Just make me like You!

Take these hands.
Take these feet.
Even these eyes,
So I can see You."

Lyrics have been taken from the song, *Mahogany Pain* by Janette ... ikz (Track 4, *Not My Own* EP)

Study

Peter continues with the same idea of suffering as he leans into the idea of understanding suffering through the form of service. Going back to verse 1 (5:1), we see that Peter draws his exhortation from his eldership, his being a witness, and his partaking of the future glory. He then goes on to tell the elders to shepherd GOD's flock and proceeds to explain how to get it done. He offers for them the same motivation that he provided for everyone earlier—the crown of glory. He then turns his attention to the younger men and quickly instructs them to be subject to their elders.

Peter ties in the overall instruction of humility for everyone, toward one another as teaching they must receive. He also uses the motivating factor of the LORD providing grace to those who humble themselves to help motivate them to the end of living humbly. He follows this with the paralleled motivation of their living under the hand of GOD.

Peter lets them know that the LORD is to be the recipient for all of their worries and concerns because He cares. They were given this responsibility because the devil was seeking to take advantage of them in order to get them to sin against the LORD. Peter commanded them to stay faithful in the midst of this suffering, for they were to know that it was limited in duration. He subsequently calls on GOD's graciousness in calling them in Christ as a witness to the finishing work that He would complete in them.

Significance

Suffering is an incredibly limited experience for the Messiah's followers. No matter how long a believer in Christ suffers, it will always come to an end. The suffering that is faced will soon be but a memory to be wiped away. We must know our Creator as being the one who holds all grace. If we truly bury this truth deep within, what we will find is the sufficiency for our souls when life seems to be too much for us. The grace that He provides us will comfort us and lead our souls to the reality that He has promised much greater than we are currently experiencing. Peter told these believers that the Lord called them to His eternal glory in Christ. This means that we are already experiencing this (which is why our perspective of suffering is impossible for the unbeliever to comprehend), but there is the greater sense of the incomprehensible magnitude of glory that is ours in the future.

The understanding that glory awaits after this life is over is an important part of the believer's suffering. We must humble ourselves to the truth that the Lord is in complete control and everything makes sense to Him, even when it doesn't make sense to us. It should bring comfort to us not to know, because many times when we think we know, we get ourselves into trouble. We must cast all of our cares, worries, and concerns upon Him, since He's the only one who can do something about them.

We must keep in mind that troubles don't last forever, and in the grand scheme, they only last for a very little while. After our time here on earth is complete, our Lord will perfect, confirm, strengthen, and establish us as we enjoy His presence forevermore.

Survey

Do you consider your earthly suffering to be only for a little while? Do you trust the Lord to be the God of all grace? Do you understand your eternal calling in Christ?

Supplication

Confess not considering your suffering to be for a little while, not trusting in the Lord's continued gracious dealings with you, and not resting your faith entirely in the Lord's eternal plan for you.

Commit to growing through the suffering that the Lord has for you and to trusting entirely in the God of all grace and His sufficiency for you.

Solicitation

We often neglect trusting the Lord in our day-to-day, but we trust Him with eternity. The truth is that it is actually easier and more convenient for us to trust Him with what we have never seen, but it becomes more difficult to trust Him in areas that we've had control over for so long. We must habitually teach ourselves to give our anxieties to Christ. He cares for us, sympathizes with us, and is able to provide exactly what we need during our times of struggle. So give Him not only your eternal hope but also your hope for today as well.

Didn't Come Here to Stay

We must understand that our lives are but a momentary existence in comparison to eternity. We must also wrestle with the reality that even if we are given many years here, these years will never compare to eternity. Therefore, if our stay here cannot compare, then we aren't seeking ultimate happiness or satisfaction here because it cannot be found in any of the created things that we enjoy.

Believer, you are not a native of this land; your home is where Christ is—represent Him well as you patiently await His return.

My Master is coming back for me, and I will be ready because I am daily preparing myself.

Therefore be on the alert, for you do not know which day your LORD is coming … For this reason you also must be ready; for the Son of Man is coming at an hour when you do not think *He will.*

Matthew 24:42, 44, NASB

"The sky rolls back as a paper scroll,
Every tongue confesses, every knee will fall,
And then I'll fly away with all who never really came here to stay."

Lyrics have been taken from the song, *Didn't Come Here to Stay* by Janette … ikz (Track 5, *Not My Own* EP)

Study

The Olivet Discourse is the last sermon that Matthew records Christ presenting. This is significant because in His last extended exposition, He shares great truths that are foundational to for believers to understand. For Christ prophesies of what is to come. The words He shares are to be internalized and adhered to.

Christ is teaching His disciples to be ready and prepared for His coming. He warns them that they must stay awake and always be ready, and He warns them in this way because they do not know the day that He is going to be coming.

He gives His disciples a small example, for them to better understand. He gives the example of the master of a home not knowing the time within the night that the thief was coming. He says that if the master of the home would have known the time the thief was coming, he would have been ready for him. Not only would he have been ready for the thief, but he also would not have allowed the thief to break into his home.

Christ goes on to point out that in like manner to this example, they too need to be watchful and ready when He returns. For He will come at a time that no one knows.

Significance

The saying goes, "When you stay ready, you don't have to get ready." This phrase is trustworthy and worthy of acceptance. We must bring ourselves to wrestle with this reality daily. We must ask ourselves the question, "Have I made myself more ready today than I was yesterday?" In our asking this question of ourselves, we force ourselves to sit with the sobering truth—whether for or against us.

When Christ commands us to be on the alert, He is commanding that always be ready, at all times. There are no off days that we can bargain for; in this way, we can never be too heavenly minded. We must be sure that we are active in doing what it is that He has instructed in His departure. Our obedience to this is how we prove we belong to Him.

This is why Christ uses the example of a thief breaking into someone's house. Whether the person was there at the time of the break-in or not is not the point. For if the master of the house knew that there was going to be a break-in at a certain time, he would have made provisions to be on the lookout at that time. But that's the main issue! We have to be on the lookout at all times, because it is impossible to know when the break-in will occur.

So we have the responsibility to have our houses in order and to be making them more prepared each day. But what does it mean to not allow for our house to be broken into? It means that we don't allow ourselves to become steeped in any sin. Because to be entrenched in any sin is to be ill-prepared for Christ's return. This is how one's home is broken into. It is because when we allow ourselves to be lulled to sleep by sin, we are no longer keeping with the vigilance that is required for our house to be in order. Our house is broken into because of our not being watchful and alert.

Survey

Do I find myself to be watchful and alert? Do I make attempts to remind myself of Christ's imminent return? Am I ready for the Son of Man's coming?

Supplication

Confess lacking in consistently remaining alert and watchful, spiritually allowing my home to be broken into, and not being ready for Christ's return.

Commit to continuously remaining prepared and watchful and to being ready for the Son of Man's coming.

Solicitation

Vigilance is something that can't simply be mustered by trying harder. It takes the Spirit of GOD to be truly watchful and aware in the ways that matter the most. We cannot do it on our own, and to try to would be foolish and a waste. We must beseech the LORD for His help and His guidance to be ready for His return. In other words, we need Him in order to be found ready for Him. This is why the command of readiness exists. It exists because He has provided the means to be ready, and all we have a responsibility to do is to trust the means he has already provided. The same spirit at work in our salvation is the same that we have to trust in our sanctification for our readiness for the Son of Man. Will you be ready—or not?

For I am confident of this very thing, that He who began a good work in you will perfect it until the day of Christ Jesus.

Philippians 1:6, NASB

"We will be like You when we see You as You are.
We wanna hear well done from our Savior and Lord."

Lyrics have been taken from the song, *Didn't Come Here to Stay* by Janette … ikz (Track 5, *Not My Own* EP)

MATTHEW WATSON

Study

Paul writes to the believers in the city of Philippi that he helped to further establish in the faith. This group was the apostle's first in Europe. This group is also known for being heavily female and very devout to the Lord. It was the habit of these women to get together to worship the Lord with one another, pray to the Father, and read and rehearse the Old Testament scriptures together. It is to these that Paul writes with such expressive joy at their continued faithfulness to the Gospel.

Paul writes to these believers, letting them know of confidence that he has about them. He tells them he is fully convinced and certain that the Lord will complete the work He began within them and that the work would be finished and brought to its end. They would continue growing in Christ until the Lord returned to call His to be with Him forevermore.

Significance

It's incredible that we as human beings are able to have confidence in anything. Many times when we place our confidence in something, our hope is shattered. Because the reality of the human experience is that we will experience disappointment in the form of both letting others down and being let down by others. But what Paul references is antithetical to the notion of disappointment.

Paul is certain of the reality of their being presented before Christ. He is sure that Christ will continue to mature them until He comes back to call them to be with Him forever. This too is our very hope, that when Christ returns, He is coming back for us. And that when we see Him, we will not have to shrink back for fear of Him, but that He will make us perfect like Himself. Because of this, we will be able to see Him as He is.

There was no hesitancy in Paul about Christ's perfecting them. This wasn't based upon any spiritual hierarchy or prominence, but faithfulness to the LORD. This should be our encouragement in the midst of all that we face in this life. We must remember that we have a responsibility to know the promises of the LORD, that we may trust in them.

Survey

Am I sure of the LORD's working within me? How does the LORD's good work within me evidence itself? Do I find myself cooperating or resisting the LORD's maturing me?

Supplication

Confess lacking in confidence about the work that the LORD began within self or another believer and not being properly motivated by the day of Christ.

Commit to fortifying your mind with scripture promises that you may be confident in the good work that the LORD has begun.

Solicitation

The journey with Christ is all about faith, for faith is how the journey begins, continues, and comes to its final completion.

This is Paul's point for us to understand when he speaks of the good work that the LORD has begun. GOD gives to us the faith to believe, and He in His faithfulness to Himself would never abandon the work that He starts. This is the promise that we are to cling to, "The LORD will never leave me nor forsake me." He started this work within each one who believes, individually, and He has provided each of us with all we need in order to continue to progress in this journey. He has also assured us that, when Christ appears, He will make us like Him. This is the hope that we ready ourselves with daily until the LORD calls us home or until the day of Christ—whichever comes first. Of this we are to be unwaveringly confident and to have placed all of our hope.

But since we are of *the* day, let us be sober, having put on the breastplate of faith and love, and as a helmet, the hope of salvation. For GOD has not destined us for wrath, but for obtaining salvation through our LORD Jesus Christ, who died for us, so that whether we are awake or asleep, we will live together with Him. Therefore encourage one another and build up one another, just as you also are doing.

1 Thessalonians 5:8-11, NASB

"Just want to make a difference,
Can't focus on the sufferin'.
GOD, He made a covenant
That when I die I live again."

Lyrics have been taken from the song, *Didn't Come Here to Stay* by Janette … ikz (Track 5, *Not My Own* EP)

Study

Paul's first letter to the Thessalonian church is written to encourage them to remain steadfast in the faith that they had been established in and were receiving immense persecution for. What we also see from Paul is further instruction on those future things that are to come and the hope that they were to have in knowing what was going to happen in the future. The eschatological (end times) issues he writes about were to be a comfort for their faithfulness to the Lord. It wasn't to be something that brought them anxiety or worry.

Paul begins his new writing point in verse 1 as chapter 5 begins. He says to them that they know the events that were to take place and that they had no need for anything new to be written to them in regard to that matter. He still decides to begin to paint a picture of what things will be like in verse 3. He quickly warns them that what he has shared in verse 3 does not pertain to them, since they are sons of light and day. Paul then continues his encouragement as he tells them of the expectation that is upon them because of their positioning in Christ.

Paul begins verse 8 with the challenge to the Thessalonians to live in a sober-minded and self-controlled way. He instructs them that they were to have placed their breastplate and helmet on themselves. The breastplate was to be of faith and love, while the helmet was to be of the hope of salvation.

Paul's rationale for their equipping themselves in this was with the motivation that they were not destined for wrath. He reiterates to them that not only was this the case, but to steady their minds upon the truth that they were destined to obtain salvation through Christ. They were to be totally committed to Him in their life as well as in their death. The responsibility that Paul gave them was to be continually strengthening, edifying, and encouraging one another, as was their practice.

Significance

We are different. It's okay to say this out loud. It's even better if you can say it with pride. We are not like the one who does not believe and lives life without hope for what comes after this life. For believers, we know that eternal life is what this life is all about. We discipline ourselves now for the overwhelming joy that we know eternity with Christ will be.

In the same way that Paul commanded the Thessalonians to be self-controlled and sober-minded, we have the same responsibility. We must be sure to equip ourselves in the same way that scripture has instructed us. In order to be successful in this, Paul points out two important pieces of equipment. The first is the breastplate of faith and love.

It's important to note that he references this same piece of armor about a decade later when he writes to the church at Ephesus. This is important to note because as he writes to them, he references the breastplate of righteousness. It's important to note that this is not a contradiction but can easily be understood in its context as different points of emphasis for differing groups. For the breastplate of righteousness, the emphasis is on the righteousness that is ours in Christ. The Father sees us as righteous, and we are protected by the righteousness that has been afforded us. The same can be said for the breastplate of faith and love, since we are protected by the faith that we have been granted by the Lord. Not only this, but we are also protected by the love that the Father has bestowed upon us as well. So in the same way that the righteousness of Christ protects us from the accuser of our souls, we are also protected in the same way by unwavering faith and unconditional love. Stated simply, the emphasis for righteousness is based upon defense from the enemy, while faith and love are based upon how we are to live unblemished by this world.

We see the same differing emphasis on the helmet, but it is a little clearer to see the similarity, since salvation is referenced in both cases. The distinction can be seen in the helmet being called the helmet of the hope of salvation to the Thessalonians, while to the believers at Ephesus, it is called the helmet of salvation. If we recall the last sentence in the previous paragraph, it will be easy for us to notice what Paul has done in these references. To the Thessalonians, Paul's point is to teach them how they must walk uprightly. He tells them that it is their hope of salvation that will keep them pure and walking as sons of light. His point to the Ephesians is that they need to stand firm against the enemy of their souls, so they needed to protect their minds from their enemy who sought to remove their confidence in Christ. Paul teaches them that they are to equip themselves with the truth of their salvation. The way we practically do this is through reminding ourselves of the truths about the Lord's choice redemption of us. Our minds become continually fortified as we remind ourselves of these truths of our salvation, and our enemy cannot penetrate our minds.

Survey

Do I live life in a self-controlled and clear-sighted way? Do I keep myself equipped in my breastplate and helmet? Is it my habit to edify and console my brothers and sisters in the faith?

Supplication

Confess lacking the sobriety and clear-mindedness necessary for a representative of Christ and not remaining properly equipped with the breastplate and the helmet.

Commit to living soberly and exercising self-control, to being consistently armored in the breastplate and helmet, and to reassuring and edifying others in the faith.

Solicitation

Our responsibility for soberness isn't a one-time commitment or something that comes and goes. Our obligation to live as children of light should permeate all of our being. It should cause us to live with a dedication to Christ that is unrivaled. As we live with this incomparable devotion, we shield ourselves from being stained by the world. It is then that our testimony of Christ to them will shine, and they will be able to see that He has made us different. This is the end that we are to be encouraging one another as we anticipate the hope of our salvation.

Let us hold fast the confession of our hope without wavering, for He who promised is faithful; and let us consider how to stimulate one another to love and good deeds, not forsaking our own assembling together, as is the habit of some, but encouraging *one another*; and all the more as you see the day drawing near.

Hebrews 10:23–25, NASB

"Some glad mornin' when this life is over,
I didn't come here to stay.
Oh, when I die
Hallelujah by and by
I really didn't come
I never really came here to stay."

Lyrics have been taken from the song, *Didn't Come Here to Stay* by Janette ... ikz (Track 5, *Not My Own* EP)

Study

The author of Hebrews writes in order to encourage those of Hebrew origin to properly understand and categorize the Messiah who had come. He's writing to them to ensure their understanding of Christ and that they didn't descend into unbelief or disbelief. Much of the writing is encouragement to those who are of the faith, but a great awareness within the letter to those who aren't yet of the faith.

Beginning at verse 19 and leading into the passage of focus, we see the writer calling these believers to live according to their confidence. He reminds them of the great truth that they were to have this confidence because of what has been accomplished on their behalf by the blood of the Messiah. He teaches them that Christ began a new way through His flesh being torn on their behalf. It was this action that granted them their confident access, since He was their high priest. He taught them that they had full access and absolute assurance of the faith that was within them. As a result of this, they were not to allow their consciences to weigh them down or allow their trust in their rituals to keep them from their treasuring what the Messiah had afforded them.

He then encourages them in holding true to their faith in the Messiah unambiguously, while reminding them of His faithfulness. Because of the truth of their faith, they had the responsibility of building a greater love and bond within their community of faith. He then provided them with a warning against neglecting their gathering together. But they had a responsibility to band together and continually be growing in their reassurance of each other.

MATTHEW WATSON

Significance

Our hope is to be built upon the faithfulness of the LORD. We were granted the ability to believe because of the faith that He granted unto us. We are to show our thankfulness for what He has done for us by not only the way that we live our lives but also based on what we are to remind ourselves of. Christ returning for all of those who love Him is the foundation of our hope. We have confessed that we believe in Him, and eternity with Him is the promised reward for this faith. We can hold tightly to this promise that He has made to us because of His proven faithfulness.

His faithfulness fuels our faithfulness to that which He has entrusted to us—each other. Whether we like it or love it, we have a huge responsibility to our brothers and sisters in the faith. Our passage introduces a few of these responsibilities to us.

The first that we see in our passage is the charge to inspire one another to love. Often love is the first to go in our pursuit of orthodoxy. It's as if we desire so much truth that we forget the love that is married to it. Love is connected to good deeds in this instruction. This is because these good works are the way we show our love. It's easy for someone to say that they love someone, but it is harder to connect that love to the performance of a good deed. But we have a responsibility to not only be examples of this, but to be such examples of this that we motivate each other to bearing this fruit.

He goes on to say that our understanding of our responsibility to one another should keep us from neglecting our gathering together. This is the core of the writer's message—the Messiah and His imminent return. We should be motivated with the return of Christ. This should help us to continuously be growing in our inspiration toward further faithfulness in Christ.

Survey

Am I faithful and resolute in my confession of Christ? Do I truly reassure others of Christ's faithfulness? Am I ready and looking forward to the day of Christ's return?

Supplication

Confess being inconsistent in your confession of hope, not placing trust in the Lord's faithfulness to His promises.

Commit to being firm and absolutely resolute in the hope that is possessed in Christ and to growing in your reassurance of others of the Lord's biblical promises.

Solicitation

We confess our hope in Christ, and we absolutely trust in it. Christ is faithful and true and always keeps His promises, no matter how dire a situation may appear. This is why He has proven worthy of our trust. But before Christ, we would trust and hope in all sorts of things that continuously brought us heartache, yet we continued to pursue those things and people. The thing about Christ, though, is that He is entirely different, but He condescends to sympathize with our condition. In taking after His perfect example, let's make it our habit to sympathize with one another. For this accountability is what's going to be necessary to grow, as we know that Christ's return is closer with each passing day.

The end of all things is near; therefore, be of sound judgment and sober *spirit* for the purpose of prayer.

1 Peter 4:7, NASB

"Let's face it, I will never be satisfied.
It's not enough.
Tell them that it's human nature.
See the things that I see,
Want the things that I want,
But I don't really need a thing."

Lyrics have been taken from the song, *Didn't Come Here to Stay* by Janette … ikz (Track 5, *Not My Own* EP)

Study

Peter's motivation is for these believers to understand the urgency of the Gospel that they have believed. He knew that he needed to motivate them toward remaining steadfast in their love for one another in the midst of the suffering and persecution that they were facing.

In our verse, Peter writes that the end has come near to them, and these believers were to have a response based on this information. They were to exercise self-control and be full of integrity. They were also to be clear-headed and restrained; all of these behaviors were for the purpose of prayer.

They were to live in this way toward one another while being committed to prayer because of the nearness of the end.

Significance

Peter writes to strangers and aliens in a foreign land that is not their own. The reality of the believer's sojourn on this earth is the same as the native reader's—the land in which we live is not our own. It's so easy for us to get caught up in this world and all the things that take place here. We can even get absorbed in the things that we can amass while we are here, all the while missing the entire purpose for our being here.

Every person has been placed on earth to seek after the LORD, pursuing the knowledge of Him until a foundation is achieved. Once this foundational knowledge is achieved, we have the responsibility to continuously be building upon it. This commitment exists with us as long as we are here on earth.

A part of this acquired knowledge about the LORD is that He is soon to return.

The nearness of the LORD's return is to be a monumental factor in our daily inspiration. It's easy for us to be compelled by the nearness of the end because of all that Christ came and accomplished. We know that He can come back at any time, and we have the charge from Him to be ready.

The end of all things being near is a motivator toward the pursuit of holiness and a repellant from ungodliness. When we think of Christ's return, we don't usually think of certain ungodly things that sometimes cross our minds. It's because we know that we wouldn't ever want Him to know those things about us or to see us in that way. But the reality is that He knows and sees all, in every scope of time—future included. In this knowledge, He still loves us and calls us His children. This is reassurance to continue to press in and pursue godliness, because in the LORD's knowledge of the future, He shows us that He hasn't given up on us.

Survey

Do I live motivated by the end of all things being near? Do I exercise restraint and self-control in all things? Do I live in a disciplined way for the purpose of prayer?

Supplication

Confess not being properly motivated by Christ's imminent return, not living in a disciplined and self-controlled manner, and not being committed to prayer.

Commit to sobering your mind for the purpose of effective prayer and to greater attentiveness in your prayer life.

Solicitation

Prayer is foundational in the believer's daily journey with Christ. This is because our prayer to Him shows our need and dependence upon Him. Since we don't know when He is going to be coming back, we must be seeking Him all the more while He is gone. For His coming is near to us, because there is nothing else that needs to take place before He returns. This truth should sober our minds and cause for us to pray that we are ready for Christ's return.

"Behold, I am coming quickly, and My reward *is* with Me, to render to every man according to what he has done."
He who testifies to these things says, "Yes, I am coming quickly." Amen. Come, Lord Jesus.

Revelation 22:12, 20, NASB

"Great is the love You have shown to us.
Great is the love You shown!"

Lyrics have been taken from the song, *Didn't Come Here to Stay* by Janette … ikz (Track 5, *Not My Own* EP)

Study

John had been given a revelation while exiled on the isle of Patmos that had differing instructions based on what was being revealed to him. The revelation he was given was prophetic and provided future instruction as well as the direction of the future course of events.

As John's revelation comes to an end in verse 10, he is instructed not to seal up the words contained in his revelation. The words were not to be sealed because of the blessing these words would be to those who would read them and the nearness of the time for their actualization. John wrote that because the time is near, people would continue their lifestyle of practice until they can't do it any longer. Those who act in an evil and wicked way will continue until they are no longer here to behave in this manner anymore. Those who are righteous will continue to live in a holy way until they are no longer on earth.

Motivation to right living can be seen in the words spoken in verse 12. Christ says that He is coming quickly and His reward will be with Him when He comes. When He comes, He will give to each one according to what was done here on earth, whether good or bad.

At the end of John's revelation, Christ Himself testifies to His swift return.

Significance

We must seek the Lord while today is today because tomorrow is not promised to anyone. The uncertainty of tomorrow should be a truth that causes any individual in the pursuit of wickedness to cease. This same truth of the uncertainty of tomorrow should motivate the one who believes to continue to fight to pursue holiness.

Another motivating factor is the understanding that Christ brings each one's return with Him. The truth about this return is that we like to use the term *reward*, but the idea is more neutral in understanding that each one will receive according to what has been earned. This is not to say that salvation can in any way be earned, but to point out that faithfulness to our time on earth matters. This reception of a return helps the believer to wrestle with routine things that could seemingly not matter. But what we see here is that the decisions after accepting Christ matter as well, because how we live as Christians makes a difference not only in this life as witnesses but also in the one to come.

Survey

Do I understand that when the LORD comes, He will return to each one according to what has been done? Do I trust that the LORD is indeed coming quickly? Do I long for His return?

Supplication

Confess not believing that the LORD will be swift in His coming and not daily anticipating the LORD's return.

Commit to being fully prepared for the LORD's coming and to desiring the LORD to come.

Solicitation

We are to have an anticipatory view of the Lord's coming. It is not simply to be some event for us; but it is to be as the excitement is for a bride coming down the aisle, adorned for her husband. Looking forward to His return is to be an exciting time and filled with mounting anticipation. As His bride, we are to desire to see Him and be united with Him forever. We should allow nothing in this world to fog or blur that reality. Our hearts should truly focus upon our rock—the rock of our salvation. Together we say, "Come, Lord. Come."